TRUE STORIES

to Remind You of Heaven
When Life Hurts Like Hell

MICHAEL BRANCH

Available on Amazon.com
and other retail outlets

Pickle Perfect Publishing
www.pickleperfectpublishing.com

Copyright © 2017 Michael Branch
All rights reserved.

ISBN: 0692914765
ISBN-13: 978-0692914762

Cover Design: Gary Brumley

Hurt

Your righteousness is righteous forever,
and Your law is true.
Trouble and anguish have found me out,
but Your commandments are my delight.
Your testimonies are righteous forever;
give me understanding that I may live.
Psalm 119:142-144

Hope

But our citizenship is in heaven,
and from it we await a Savior, the Lord Jesus Christ,
who will transform our lowly body to be like
His glorious body, by the power that enables Him
even to subject all things to Himself.
Philippians 3:20-21

Contents

Rules, Rules, Rules

Faith and Works

Marvelous Me

A Joyful Noise

Road Trip

Holidays

Getting Personal

True Freedom

Hurting, Hope, Heaven

Before you start. Each story opens with a verse of Scripture. If you're like me, you will be tempted to jump past that and go straight into the story. Here is my recommendation: Read the verse first. The Word of God is the foundation on which everything else rests. Without it, the stories are all meaningless.

Introduction

*Let all the earth fear the LORD; let all the inhabitants
of the world stand in awe of Him! Psalm 33:8*

One morning, 800 people at our company were called into meetings in far-flung cities to hear some startling news: We were losing our jobs.

For a good 15 minutes the formal announcement left me breathless and unbelieving. It reminded me of the moment when I first broke a bone – a common injury that I managed to avoid until I was nearly 40. Not somebody else's bone, but mine! I couldn't believe it. Other people break their bones. Other people lose their jobs. And across the land other people face bankruptcy. Other people hear their doctors say "cancer." Other people . . . .

But it's not just other people, is it? Sometimes it's your turn to be the other people. And that's when you find out where your faith really lies.

The God I know is faithful in every moment of life – whether in times we call "good" or times we call "bad." In the stories that follow, you will quickly learn about the God who first loved us so that we might come to love Him.

But first a word about how I came to write these stories. Several years ago an individual at our company started an email group to distribute a daily Nugget – a quick expression of God's Word sown among anyone who wanted to join the list. The group grew, and I joined as a recipient. Then God, in His providence, opened the door to my becoming a contributor. The stories you see here are a few of those insights that God spoke into my heart to share as Nuggets through the years.

The Monday after our company left us breathless, I wrote a note to some of my coworkers comparing our layoffs to the winding down of a carousel. I called it Monday on the Merry Go Round, and I have included it in this book. The response surprised me. One man urged me to share my writing more broadly. A woman came by my cubicle, planted herself on a corner of my desk, and said, "I'm serious about this. You need to write a book. Seriously." I think most writers hear that well-meaning suggestion at one time or another, and my inclination is to shrug it off. But this time it seemed different. This time it seemed like the right time. So . . . this is it.

Most of these stories begin with life's littlest moments – something I have observed in my life or someone else's. Everybody's life consists of such moments, strung together from the time you wake up until you crawl back into bed at night. The question is, what do you see in them?

Everywhere I look I see God's big plan working itself out. It's called the Gospel. Our lives are a front row seat to the awesome ways and being of our Creator, Sustainer, and Redeemer in which we are both actor and audience. By grace, this is how I see the world. I pray that you, with practice and the Spirit through whom God makes His Son known, take courage as you too see Him in life's littlest moments yourself. Your life's littlest moments.

Look closely. God is always there, worthy of your wonder and awe, even in your hurt.

Tears
Testing
Triumph

Hurting in Life
Hoping in Heaven

Hurting in Life

I will be with you. I will not leave you or forsake you.
Joshua 1:5b

"Go away." My company used different words the day it communicated its intention to lay off hundreds of people, but that was the message my heart heard. "Changing direction" and "staffing in different ways" were statements of fact. "You have no place here" was a statement of life.

I suddenly relived a call from several years earlier.

Our family business had been crushed by the economy, and we had racked up a mountain of debt trying to weather the storm. We had raided personal savings, liquidated other investments, and pulled from funds earmarked for inheritance to keep the company afloat. As a primary owner, I was on the hook for all of it. The outlook was grim, but we held fast to our faith in God. He had brought the company through rough times before in its 100-year history.

Then my brother called. After several years of surviving on daily negotiations with creditors, it was over. No more denial. No more hope against hope. Just a huge weight dropping into my stomach, taking every measure of oxygen with it. It was about a legacy, it was about our 100+ employees, it was about our family's future. It was about bankruptcy and the loss of all certainty. Adding to the weight was the fact that some of the debt was to the government, which even bankruptcy wouldn't cover. I was also facing treatment for Lyme Disease, and two major issues as an elder at our church.

We did make it through those hard times . . . one minute, hour, and day at a time. Another company preserved many jobs for our employees, at least for awhile. And our mighty, merciful, strong and gentle God even worked out the government debt so that we were not left with its burden. But these were grueling, agonizing years full of unknowns.

I went from corner office, to jobless, to contract work, to cubicle. My wife and I went from large house in a prosperous neighborhood to nice cookie-cutter house half the size. When our last child moved out my wife went back to the workplace.

And . . . we experienced the most urgent and intimate walk with Christ in our lives.

Nothing drives you to the cross like a need for God – not a need for riches or having things your way, but a need for Him! A need for a loving lap to crawl into, mighty arms to hold you fast, assurance that you are not forgotten, a promise that you have purpose, a knowledge that every failure of yours has been covered. As surely as God took care of my inescapable government debt, He paid for my unforgivable sins.

I was breathless when I heard I had been rejected by my company. But then I remembered how God has carried me through breathless times before, only to set me down in even better places.

If I were still at our family business, I would never have felt the same kinds of hurt. I would never have begun to capture stories that speak of God's grace. I would never have written this book. I would never have drunk so deeply of Christ with people I met along the way. I would never have breathed God in the same way.

When I think of what God has done, I am breathless again. He lives! He cares! He rescues! He redeems! He sets my feet upon a Rock for my good and for His glory! And He uses even hurt to shape me (and you) into someone who relies on Him more than ever.

Today. Remember that God gave you breath. Then ask Him to help you appreciate that He sometimes empties your lungs so that He may refill them with the purity of His kindness, the knowledge of His grace, and the joy of His presence and promise.

The Gospel. By surrendering His own breath on the cross, Jesus made Himself to be your sure foundation in every circumstance. *For You are my rock and my fortress; and for Your Name's sake You lead me and guide me. Psalm 31:3*

Hoping in Heaven

*By the sweat of your face you shall eat bread, till you return
to the ground, for out of it you were taken;
for you are dust, and to dust you shall return. Genesis 3:19*

It was hot, sweaty work. My muscles ached from lifting the massive metal rod again. And again. And again.

Each time I pounded the rod into the earth my hands stung with the painful shock of hardened metal striking unrelenting rock. It was a grueling activity, all so I could move a sprinkler head out from behind a new stretch of fence I had built.

All I needed was 14 feet of trench 10 inches deep, but my earth was populated with rocks. Huge rocks. Hard rocks. Deep rocks. Just when I thought I was home free I'd hit another stubborn obstacle. What would have been a pleasant 20 minute job in cultivated earth took hours of sustained pounding. Most times my effort seemed to yield nothing. Then I would finally sense a crack in the rock below and feel some progress. Chip by chip the rocks yielded ground.

Finally, I blasted through the last few inches to reach the spot where I needed to plant the sprinkler head. I couldn't believe what I saw! Just one inch from my final destination lay an underground irrigation pipe. If I had known it was there, I could have simply dug one little hole to tap into the line with my new head. I could have avoided the whole rocky path my trench had taken and the arduous hours of work. If I'd only known.

I knelt there for a minute, dumbfounded. Crusted in dirt, sweaty and weary, I considered my choices. I could cry about it or I could appreciate the irony. I could resent the journey or I could celebrate my effort. I could curse the earth or I could remember something God revealed long ago: The earth was already cursed. My inclination to rebel against Him had led to all of earth's countless troubles. In the Garden of Eden mankind had the opportunity to enjoy access to God's eternal flow of living water forever. And we blew it. So God sent us the long way around.

We have some friends whose life journey looks just like my trenching experience. For decades their lives have kept hitting one rock after another. Honestly, it doesn't seem fair or just. The pains seem to line up in a queue, never leaving time for one to yield before the next one steps in to take its place. They don't do anything overt to deserve their troubles. They work hard. They spend wisely. They worship faithfully. Yet, like Job, there seems to be no end to the troubles they endure. Health fails, jobs fall through, finances waver, supportive relationships falter.

It's a puzzling dilemma, and I don't propose a simple answer. Every bit of human reasoning breaks down. But the fact remains, the God who could save my friends from the troubles of a lifetime spent digging out rocks hasn't done so.

You might feel the same way. You feel like Job, whose losses suddenly outweigh his gains. You feel like Job who – it turns out – God was using to demonstrate the difference that trusting in Him makes in a human soul. Seen from the earth side, Job is a story about human heartache. But seen from the heaven side, Job is a story where God baffles the devil's efforts to destroy what God chooses to preserve.

All of heaven watched as God empowered and sustained Job to withstand the effects of sin in the world! All of heaven wondered at Job's resilience, even as he struggled with failing health, wavering finances, and the collapse of supportive relationships! Job struggled. Job hurt. Job took the long and rocky way around. Yet Job triumphed because God was with him. As he did so, heavenly beings looked on in awe at who God was and what He accomplished in Job's life!

In the end, Job's fortunes were restored and multiplied. *See Job 42*. That doesn't mean you will find that same thing on your painful earthly journey, but it does point you to what God has in mind for you in heaven.

In Matthew 5, Jesus promises: *"Blessed are the poor in spirit, for theirs is the kingdom of heaven. Blessed are those who mourn, for they shall be comforted. Blessed are the meek, for they shall inherit the earth. Blessed are those who hunger and thirst for righteousness, for they shall be satisfied. Blessed are the merciful, for they shall receive mercy. Blessed are the pure in heart, for they shall see God. Blessed are the peacemakers, for they shall be called sons of God. Blessed are those who are persecuted for righteousness' sake, for theirs is the kingdom of heaven. Blessed are you when others revile you and persecute you and utter all kinds of evil against you falsely on my account. Rejoice and be glad, for your reward is great in heaven, for so they persecuted the prophets who were before you."*

Today. Job's hurt was not purposeless. Job's faithfulness was not without reward. Your journey may be long, rocky and painful. But when sweat burns your eyes and your muscles fail – when all hope of digging one more inch seems impossible – remember this: In Christ, your journey leads back to the source of the Fountain of Life. God's angels are watching the out-working of His impossible redemption of your soul from the curse that still haunts your days on earth. But that's not forever. Step into the next few pages and be reminded of God's work. Be reminded of His plan. And be reminded of heaven, where only one Rock remains – your Savior Jesus Christ.

The Gospel. The blood of Christ has overcome the curse that left us hopeless and counting on our own efforts to dig for living water. He gives us the Holy Spirit as our comfort and strength. And to what end? Listen to the Good News promised in this parable: *"His master said to him, 'Well done, good and faithful servant. You have been faithful over a little; I will set you over much. Enter into the joy of your master.'" Matthew 25:23* There is hope in what lies ahead. God calls it heaven.

Courage
and
Contentment

Bankrupt
Story Time
Meltdown
Only 3 More Strikes
Pain and Promise
Blessed are the Pour
Worth Weighting For

Bankrupt

*According to His great mercy, He has caused us to be born again
to a living hope through the resurrection of Jesus Christ
from the dead, to an inheritance that is imperishable, undefiled,
and unfading, kept in heaven for you. 1 Peter 1:3-4*

A few weeks ago, a constable appeared on my neighbor's doorstep to serve an eviction notice. My neighbor had no hope of repaying his debts. They foreclosed on his residence and dragged his other worldly goods into the front yard. It was a sad moment for my neighbor and for the neighborhood. By the time I took this picture some remnants of his life were already loaded into vehicles of strangers who passed by.

So what do you see in this picture? I see a man's spirit crushed, a house emptied, and worldly possessions scattered. I see an inheritance perishing, defiled, and fading away.

"Bankrupt" is one way of saying, "It's all gone." That may

be what your hurt feels like. Something you value is gone or seems to be slipping away. It leaves you feeling empty, crushed, and scattered. That's a terrible feeling, even for a short time in this life on earth.

But what if bankruptcy on earth is just a glimpse that God gives us of something much bigger and eternal? We are all, in fact, spiritually bankrupt. Nothing we possess – good works, good intentions, or even good sufferings – is the right currency to make our debts (called sins) right with God. None of our debts are hidden from him, and every effort to cover for them is useless. That is pain on a cosmic level.

We are separated from His eternal life unless we accept a payment that only He can supply, the blood of Christ. He offers it freely, knowing every sin that it covers.

In fact, God knows all things, even the hurts you think are going unnoticed. He is caring for you in ways you may not see. He is working in you changes you may not feel. It is the same all-knowingness that lets Him see every way in which we need a Savior.

When I see someone who knows Jesus, I see a person's spirit made new, an eternal home prepared, and an inheritance that is not subject to seizure, to scattering, or to spoil. That is the hope of heaven, an incomparable treasure.

Today. What walls and roof are you counting on to protect your happiness, and what possessions are keeping you content? Think about what would happen if you lost them all – then be thankful again that Christ's riches are laid up in heaven for you.

The Gospel. *In [Christ] we have redemption through His* *blood, the forgiveness of our trespasses, according to the riches of His grace, which He lavished upon us, in all wisdom and insight making known to us the mystery of His will, according to His purpose, which He set forth in Christ as a plan for the fullness of time, to unite all things in Him, things in heaven and things on earth. Ephesians 1:7-10*

Story Time

Jesus wept. John 11:35

Does your heart tell you stories? Mine does.

Last week traffic was at a standstill on the interstate, and a pickup caught my eye. A couple of kids' beds were tied down in the back – one pink and pretty, the other blue and gnarly. Finally the traffic loosened up and the truck got ahead of me by 100 yards or so. Then, to my horror, a tie-down must have slipped on the truck. That pretty pink bed suddenly flew out onto the highway.

My mind flashed to my granddaughters and their beds, and how some little girl was going to find out that the bed she loved was destroyed. Cars were swerving all around; the truck was desperately moving toward the shoulder. And my heart told me a story about some broken-hearted child whose precious pink night-comfort was gone. I felt her hurt. I couldn't stop thinking about it.

My heart made up that story that temporarily crushed my soul, but what if I knew the real story? What if I knew the real story about everybody – about how much hidden hurt and pain people carried around? About how joy could have been theirs if they made different choices? About beauty they might behold if they just looked up?

Jesus knew. Jesus' heart told Him real stories because He knew everybody's hearts. All day He saw people as they truly were, hopeless and without a Shepherd. He saw them with His human eyes, and with His divine heart.

Jesus knows your story, too – not just a story His heart makes up, but the real story based on every nook and cranny of your past history and your unspent future.

Most of all, He knows your sin. He became your sin. He became the very root of your brokenness. Then He carried that to the cross.

Today. Grasp that truth and you have begun to grasp the Bible. Grasp that and you have begun to grasp the Savior. Grasp that and you will let your heart tell you the story of Jesus over and over and over. Every other story where you want to rescue somebody from heartbreak – it's just a shadow of Jesus' real redemption story. How will you see people (and yourself) differently today?

The Gospel. God became man and rewrote the story of every person who believes His message of repentance and clings to Him as Redeemer and Lord. His last words on the cross were "The End" ("it is finished") – which turns out to be the opening line in the Book of Life.

Meltdown

The steadfast love of the Lord never ceases;
His mercies never come to an end. Lamentations 3:22

I don't remember why I was reaching into the refrigerator

freezer a few weeks ago, but I do remember what came out. Mushy ice cream. Mushy everything. We tried some basic fixes for the appliance, like vacuuming the coils and resetting the breaker. Meanwhile we loaded some store-bought ice inside to maintain the cool.

The problem with ice is that it works great at first – but then it melts!

Within 48 hours the refrigerator/freezer was warm and lifeless. We loaded the contents into ice chests where the ice again worked great at first, but kept melting. We kept purcha$ing and reloading ice until we could get a new appliance. In the end, the ice chests weren't nearly cool enough.

I was ecstatic when we finally got that refrigerator replaced after a few days. Not only did it maintain the right temperature, but the energy and money required to keep replenishing ice for the chests were really wearing us down!

What does that have to do with our lives and salvation? Well, we inherently understand that there is a healthy standard we need to meet in our lives. But the only way we can imagine to naturally meet the standard is to work harder and harder – and our efforts just seem to melt away as soon as we do them. Every religion is built on that principle (good works applied over and over again) except for one. Aren't you glad you know Jesus?

Are you hurting? Turn to Him.

Are you striving after "more ice," only to see it melt away as your focus and energy waver? Come to Him.

Are you overcome by the burden of thinking that your works somehow contribute to or earn your salvation? Rest instead in Him.

Jesus is your only preservation. With unceasing love, He sends new manna every day to feed your soul. Your good works are to be a reflection of His love working in you, not a means to attract His affection. Good works can be ice He gives you to bring Him honor, not the means by which His blessings are earned.

Today. Jesus says, *"Come to Me, all who labor and are heavy laden, and I will give you rest." Matthew 11:28*

The Gospel. While we were still choosing to spoil in the heat of our own sin, Jesus bore the cross to become a sustaining sanctuary. By His blood our lives are saved, and by His Spirit we are preserved to the end.

Only 3 More Strikes

*When the servant of the man of God rose early in the morning
and went out, behold, an army with horses and chariots
was all around the city. And the servant said,
"Alas, my master! What shall we do?" 2 Kings 6:15*

At the ballpark one night, my granddaughter was rooting for the Texas Rangers. She learned how to look at the scoreboard to see how many balls and strikes the pitcher had thrown to a batter and how many of each it took before the player went to first base or was called "out."

In one case she saw that the count on the opposing batter was 3 balls and 0 strikes – a real long shot to strike out the batter, for sure! But she was blind to the odds.

"Hey," she shouted, "We only need three more strikes!" And she was right.

At one point the prophet Elisha found himself surrounded by a huge Syrian army determined to capture him. All his servant saw was the staggering odds against him.

But Elisha saw the situation with different eyes. The Lord showed him that the Syrians were doomed to defeat – because the Lord had already declared victory for His people. Elisha said, *"Do not be afraid, for those who are with us are more than those who are with them." Then Elisha prayed and said, "O Lord, please open his eyes that he may see." So the Lord opened the eyes of the young man, and he saw, and behold, the mountain was full of horses and chariots of fire all around Elisha. 2 Kings 6:16-17* God's army had always been greater than the Syrian army.

Does your own hurt seem overwhelming? Satan would like to hide the reality of God's purpose, power and design from your eyes. He would like you to see evil in control of the game, with no chance of striking it out. But take heart today and always! Although there may be dark innings, Jesus has already delivered the winning pitches on your behalf.

Today. Root with confidence, believer! See with your Jesus eyes. The game is already decided. Christ's blood has already overcome all earthly odds, negating every error that had been rightfully held against you.

The Gospel. *For everyone who has been born of God overcomes the world. And this is the victory that has overcome the world – our faith. Who is it that overcomes the world except the one who believes that Jesus is the Son of God? 1 John 5:4-5*

Pain and Promise

Have I not commanded you? Be strong and courageous.
Do not be frightened, and do not be dismayed,
for the Lord your God is with you wherever you go. Joshua 1:9

When our first foster child came to live with us, we built a window cornice for his room. It was in the shape of a rainbow, complete with bright stripes and puffy cotton clouds – a tangible expression of a promise-keeping God. Later we began collecting other Noah's Ark themed pieces. The rainbow broke off one of those pieces a few years ago. It still hasn't reached the top of my list to fix, I'm afraid. It's not causing me enough pain to worry about.

Pain matters. It pushes priorities to the top: marriages in trouble, distress over finances, cancer. We all know people who are dealing in earnest with things like that right this minute. It may even be you.

Pain matters because it means that something is broken. And worst of all, I think, is the pain from a broken promise.

Good n ews! God's Word is built on pain-relieving promises.

We are reminded about one of God's promises by the rainbow He sets in the sky, which followed His determination to save some out of the many who had turned their backs on Him. *See Genesis 8:21-22.*

Another promise also speaks of saving some out of the many who turn their backs on Him – that God did not send His Son into the world to condemn the world, but to save the world through Him. *See John 3:16-17.*

Being "in Christ" gives believers a different way to handle earth's pains. We can face perils on earth because God promises

He will care for His creation (and especially His children) day after day. We can face perils of death because God promises our lives find ultimate purpose through Him, forever.

The world is broken and full of pain. But God's promises have taken that into consideration. "Rainbows" created from man-made materials, ideas and designs will fail. But God's promises endure forever.

Today. You may be facing the pains that are inevitable in life – those set in motion by your own sins or others' sins in a fallen world. But they are not forever. God promises to relieve those pains in His time, and He has already taken the pains on Himself that make it possible.

The Gospel. The curse of sin and death is washed away by Christ for those who place their trust in Him instead of themselves. Only He is able to satisfy the requirement for righteousness that can bring God's creatures into His loving presence forever.

Blessed are the Pour

Then [Jesus] rose and rebuked the winds and the sea,
and there was a great calm. Matthew 8:26

As we thought about fixing up our house to sell a few years ago, repairs were uppermost in my mind. (Well, right behind my two daughters' upcoming weddings.) So I was stunned to discover that our roof was leaking. This meant urgently finding a pot to catch the dripping water while I called the insurance company. Later that day, I was further stunned to find that our detached carport roof was leaking. This meant frantically moving and repacking some boxes that were sitting there in the water and another call to the insurance company. We also needed to replace the fence. And repaint. And . . . .

"When it rains it pours®" is a slogan that Morton Salt adopted many years ago. It means their salt pours freely, even in high humidity, when salt tends to cling together and not pour. They wanted you to know that their salt stands the test.

From a Morton Salt perspective, that's a good thing. From a God perspective, that downpour may be the best thing. It can demonstrate our best God-shaped qualities. And when the storm clears, perhaps it even brings out our friends to be our rainbows. One such friend stepped forward to spearhead replacing our fence! God promises that He will not overflood us beyond our capacities to survive when we cry out to Him.

Today. Whatever your storms today, the Captain stands ready to hear your cries. He will see you through them. He will help you stand the test – and thereby prove the work He has done in you, for His glory. What could be better than that?

The Gospel. God pours better than the rain: *For this is my blood of the covenant, which is poured out for many for the forgiveness of sins. Matthew 26:28* In my restless soul, there is now a calm that cannot be unsettled.

Worth Weighting For

Take My yoke upon you, and learn from Me, for I am gentle and lowly in heart, and you will find rest for your souls.
Matthew 11:29

In the battle against non-fitness, my wife and I hired a mercenary, a trainer. His task was to heap more on us than we could bear, then encourage our bodies to do more than our minds thought we could do.

At one session he had me doing bench presses. We started at one weight, then he gradually put on more weight for additional sets. With eyes clenched shut, I would exert all my effort into each lift. By my amazing powers I punched more and more weight into the sky! At least I thought the power was mine, until I opened my eyes.

There was my trainer, standing above me. His hands were also on the bar. When I could no longer bear the weight, he was there to make my wholehearted effort successful. He gave me more than I could do, then he helped me do it when my strength was spent.

Have you ever heard someone say, "God will not give you more than you can bear?" They are probably well intentioned, but the Bible tells a different story.

God constantly gives people more than they can bear, beginning with a sin nature that can never break out of its cycle of imperfection. Your burden is overwhelming. By grace, He gives you opportunities to rely solely on Him, including trusting Him for your salvation. The not-without-God pattern is played out in your circumstances every day through things like challenging relationships, loss of those dear to us, financial catastrophe, or disappointing outcomes.

Though you give it all you've got, your got is not enough – without a bar-holding, care-giving, life-sustaining Savior. With every crushing weight, God provides believers with His hand on the bar, lifting what we cannot.

Today. Rely on the Savior alone today, and not on your own strength. With His yoke comes His assurance that you cannot fail in your pursuit of the life to come, which is the ultimate rest for your soul.

The Gospel. Jesus said, *"All things have been handed over to Me by My Father, and no one knows the Son except the Father, and no one knows the Father except the Son and anyone to whom the Son chooses to reveal Him. Come to Me, all who labor and are heavy laden, and I will give you rest. Take My yoke upon you, and learn from Me, for I am gentle and lowly in heart, and you will find rest for your souls. For My yoke is easy, and My burden is light." Matthew 11:27-30*

In Plain Sight

Wonder Island
Just for You
Pepper Uppers
Dirty Windows

Wonder Island

At that time Jesus declared, "I thank You, Father, Lord of heaven and earth, that You have hidden these things from the wise and understanding and revealed them to little children." Matthew 11:25

Walmart's crowded aisles can be a special testing ground for people with small children. My wife and I were trying to hurry toward the exit with a couple of distractible grandchildren when one of them suddenly dropped to the floor. What in the world? From her vantage point she had spotted an under-bench mirror in the shoe department. She was delighted. Her brother joined her at the small island of wonder hidden in Walmart's roiling sea of merchandise.

They huddled on the floor, mesmerized by the image they had discovered. I was a bit mesmerized myself. How many times had I passed this way and never recognized this bench or its hidden treasure? But there it was, revealed to some little children whose minds were not preoccupied with pre-programmed "wisdom and understanding."

I saw the stormy sea.
They saw the tiny island.
And, for a moment,
Jesus calmed the sea while His children gazed.

Rejoice that Christ alone placed your soul in a position where you would see Him! He put you on the right spiritual aisle, at the right moment, and directed your gaze. He revealed Himself to you, though to many He was hidden under a bench.

Did you notice these things about the picture? First, one child is kneeling; the other is lying on the ground. It takes humility to draw close to the Revelation of Christ. Second, the mirror is tilted just right. Peering into the island shows the children the sea from a new perspective, from floor to shelves to ceiling, even as Christians see the world in a different way through Christ.

Today. May Christ cause you to see Him anew in the course of your life today, as well. May you stop and gaze in wonder, thankful for a calm in the sea so you may glimpse and glorify Him.

The Gospel. We are told that Jesus often healed the eyes of those who could not physically see. They had no idea what they were missing. In the same way, we have no idea of Christ or our need for Him unless He heals our spiritual blindness. By grace you come to see yourself as you are, which opens your eyes to your need for a Savior.

Just for You

The heart of man plans his way,
but the Lord establishes his steps. Proverbs 16:9

My six-year-old granddaughter was darting about the church courtyard with her friends when she suddenly screeched to a halt. Reaching down, she picked up a single leaf. "Here," she said, handing it to me. "Can I take this to my science teacher?"

There she was, running full throttle with her friends when a leaf caught her eye and stopped her in her tracks. Everybody else walked over it, but she saw what God placed there and God showed her its purpose.

That leaf was for her. So were myriad other things that day, meticulously placed by God in her path: family to wake her, cereal to eat, cartoon characters to watch, a car seat to ride in, a car game to challenge her, teachers to guide her thinking, friends to delight her, and a plain brown leaf lying on the ground just for her.

The God who sets the stars in the heavens and knows each one surely knows your own hurting footsteps today. Like the parent who hides Easter eggs in plain sight right where she knows her toddler will walk, God has strewn your path with good things to please you, challenge you, and excite you.

Meeting a coworker on the stairs is not by coincidence. Victory in a project or even roadblocks galore are equally God's working on your soul. He designs each thing you see, hear or otherwise experience – huge or tiny – for a purpose.

What will you do with the leaves you find – the ones just for you – to spend on a precise moment and place in life? How will you see them differently because you know Him?

Today. What has God placed on your path, just for you?

The Gospel. Jesus' path took Him to many places in His 30-plus years in flesh, but finally to a cross where only His blood could serve to bring sinners to repentance and cover their sins. The Redeemer who said "follow Me" is the guide who leads you on His path and provides every good thing for you to enjoy and share.

Pepper Uppers

Or do you not know that your body is a temple of the Holy Spirit within you, whom you have from God? 1 Corinthians 6:19a

In the course of making daily lunch salads, I have hacked up more peppers than I can remember. But I do remember one pepper in particular. As I cut this pepper in half, I noticed the

image of joy embedded in its deepest parts.

No matter how its body might have looked on the outside, that image was preserved in its core. It was an image of joy. Can you see that smile?

Does that remind you of something? The Holy Spirit is permanently embedded inside of you, and He is the seal of Good News! Are you troubled? Are you pained? Does hope seem far away?

Take a deep breath, and remember that there is a Hope who lives within you. He is your Rock, your Core, your Joy. He is your Good News, and the Salt that makes you light. He connects to the Stem who leads to life. Whether you feel Him today or not, He never leaves you as He leads your steps, guards your ways, exercises your soul, massages your hurts, and preserves your joy.

When you wonder how God feels about those He has saved, remember His face. He is smiling, delighting in the fruit of His own impossible, transformative work in your nature. He is smiling today, tomorrow and forever.

Today. Smile, child of God. He loves you more than you can imagine.

The Gospel. *[Be] strengthened with all power, according to His glorious might, for all endurance and patience with joy; giving thanks to the Father, who has qualified you to share in the inheritance of the saints in light. Colossians 1:11-12*

Dirty Windows

He has delivered us from the domain of darkness and transferred us to the kingdom of His beloved Son, in whom we have redemption, the forgiveness of sins.
Colossians 1:13–14

One morning I saw water spots on my bathroom window, caught in the direct morning sunlight. "Arghh!" I thought. "I just cleaned that window!" Then God stepped in and changed my perspective – twice.

First, I saw that my gaze was fixed on the window surface itself. The window existed to let in light and offer a view, and I missed the joy when I focused on the spots. I missed the sunbeams. I missed the sky. I missed the purpose.

Second, I saw the marvelous way the spots got there. My sprinkler system had wet the top of the air conditioner, whose fan blew water onto the window. The spots appeared because my other systems were working behind the scenes. My yard was drinking; my inside environment was cooling.

Do you ever focus on the surface of your life – your circumstances? Good or bad, the circumstances can distract you from experiencing the joy of God's light in your life.

They can steal your focus from viewing the amazing vistas of God's love. They can keep you from recognizing that your very existence may be the result of a life well watered and an environment made bearable by God's own hand. Or ... they can make you thankful that you have been delivered from darkness.

Christ-sightedness makes things light.

Today. Look past the surfaces in your life today ... and see all the beautiful things God is providing!

The Gospel. The world walked in all-consuming darkness until Jesus Christ revealed Himself to us. *In Him was life, and the life was the light of men. John 1:4* But even after He lifts our darkness and leads us to repent of our sins, the ways of the world may distract us from remembering the depths of His love – which never ceases to exist.

Lord
of
Love

Footprints
Trash to Treasure

Footprints

*For to this you have been called, because Christ also suffered
for you, leaving you an example, so that you might
follow in His steps. 1 Peter 2:21*

I'm a Texas boy, and when I see snow I think, "Go back north where you belong." Nonetheless, the Lord knows better than I and He sometimes shares the shivers with me. On one such occasion, I gave my wife a ride so she could open the store where she worked. It was a slushy, slippery drive indeed.

A few minutes later she sent me a text with this picture. "Look what you left me in the parking lot!" she said. Sure enough, my car tracks left an early valentine. Could I do it again? Probably not. I have no idea how it happened. Some people might say it was a miracle – the kind of thing they used to show on TV shows like *Miracle Pets* or *Touched by an Angel*.

Something's a miracle all right, but it's not the hearts carved out of parking lot slush. The miracle is the love that makes the hearts-picture meaningful. The miracle is that we (who live in a world where every heart is born to harbor selfishness, greed and hatred) can imagine love at all. Though it is foreign to our fallen nature, God still chooses to let us glimpse and taste the love with which He loves us, pure and holy.

Wherever God steps He leaves an imprint of perfect love, like heart-shaped footprints. Can you believe that He is the Author of love? Can you see His footprints in your life? Can you thank Him that He shows you His love at all? Can you follow His steps to draw closer to Him?

Jesus paid a price beyond imagining to place His physical footprints on the same earth where we walk, then gave us the desire and the power to follow Him. Love Him with all your heart, soul, mind, and strength. Love others with the same commitment and intensity with which you love yourself.

Today. There is no lovelier path to take than the one that follows Christ. Look for the footprints, and treasure each one.

The Gospel. There was no costlier path for Jesus to walk than the one that took Him to the cross. He came face to face with God's rightful anger for the sins we have committed throughout our lives. For a moment He exchanged His righteousness (white as snow) for our sin (dark and hidden), so it might be possible to exchange our sin for His righteousness.

Trash to Treasure

We love because [Christ] first loved us. 1 John 4:19

"Do you want to make cookies for the man in the trash truck?" my wife asked the two-year-old grandchildren one day. "Yes! Yes! Yes!" they squealed. So they did.

When she heard the unmistakable sound of the big truck approaching, she grabbed the kids and lifted them up to the truck window to present the driver with the plate of cookies. The same scenario played out a number of times, and at Christmas we began sharing a loaf of strawberry bread as well.

It was always rushed. Trash men have no time to stop and chat; they are measured by the ground they cover on their routes. Nonetheless you could tell he was pleased. He would toot his horn as he passed and wave when he saw us outside, even on days we were too rushed to bake cookies.

He felt the love.

It was at least a year before I connected our trash man with the fact that our trash container was mysteriously moved from the street to the side of our house when it was emptied. I assumed my helpful next door neighbor was doing it. Then I happened to be home one day when the truck came by, and behold – in spite of his need to spend as little time as possible at each address he was personally taking the time to pull on his safety vest, jump out of the truck, roll our container to the house, run back to the truck, pull off his vest, and continue his rounds.

He loved us back.

Love begets love. Why? Because, like all good things, it reflects the reality of who God is and what God does.

"I am Love," says the Lord of Hosts. "I showed you what love looks like when I personally experienced temptations like yours, then received the horrible consequences of your countless sins to haul off your trash. Now I walk with you every day in pursuit of My purposes."

Love is personal. Love draws our affections. Love never

fails. What a blessing to be loved by God and to love Him in return!

Today. Who are you loving with the love of Christ – so they can feel His love and love Him back?

The Gospel. _For God so loved the world, that He gave His only Son, that whoever believes in Him should not perish but have eternal life. John 3:16_

On the Grow

Terrible Twos
Measure Up
By Gum

Terrible Twos

Brothers, do not be children in your thinking.
Be infants in evil, but in your thinking be mature. 1 Corinthians 14:20

Standing by me in the kitchen one day, my granddaughter said, "I wish I was two years old."

"Why is that?" I asked.

"Well, two year olds sometimes cry."

Pause . . .

"And two year olds sometimes try to get their own way."

Longer pause . . .

"And two year olds sometimes get candy." Then she giggled.

That was random. But it was also telling. Do you wish you

had more permission to pity yourself? Do you want your own way? Do you crave what's sweet for the moment but spiritually unhealthy in excess?

Two-year-olds help us see sin for what it is – an all-consuming obsession with Me. Truth be told, we are all still two years old on the inside. And that is about the terriblest it can ever get, defying our heavenly Father and rejecting our dependence on His Son's completed redemptive work.

No matter how much we grow in years, there is still a part of that two-year-old rebellion inside. We were born with it. That's also true of our spiritual lives, even after Christ cracks open our hard hearts and gives us a new Life. We are all on a spiritual growth journey for the rest of our earthly years as Christ conforms our lives to His.

Today. Look closely at yourself. Where are you being two years old today? That's where Christ wants to make His next change in you. And – by His grace alone – that change is actually possible and ultimately accomplished.

The Gospel. Our sin is in-born, so Christ was flesh-born, so by His perfect life and sacrifice alone we may be reborn.

Measure Up

Yet we know that a person is not justified by works of the law but through faith in Jesus Christ. Galatians 2:16a

Last week, my grandson was playing with the tape measure my wife uses for sewing. Suddenly he handed it to her with these instructions: "See how strong I am!"

She wasn't quite sure what to do next. You don't measure

strong in inches. He had his relationships mixed up. He was after something that could not be achieved.

Many people see the world in that childish way. They want to be measured for God-worthiness based on their good works. They toil hard at religious works (do this thing, this way, at this time), or moral works (guard your character, follow the law), or philanthropy (support a good cause).

But no matter how well they perform, they strive in vain.

God doesn't measure God-worthiness based on good works at all. Instead, He measures the heart. He sees that even our religious works can become idols of ritual and tradition. Our moral works often reinforce pride in a false purity. Our philanthropy is too often about making us feel good about our own generosity.

Performance appraisals at work are a great place to document your good works. That's the right measure for the right thing. But when it comes to pleasing God, that's not the way. The only way to measure up is to count on the works that Jesus has already completed perfectly and satisfactorily.

I wish I could totally shake off that warped idea of measuring my works. My sin nature keeps wanting to drag me back to the law I cannot satisfy. Maybe you have that same feeling.

Today. Look to Christ alone, who relieves us of the impossible standard of measuring whether we are tall enough to reach Him. Depend instead on His nail-scarred hand to reach low enough to pull you up.

The Gospel. *For, being ignorant of the righteousness of God, and seeking to establish their own, they did not submit to God's* *righteousness. For Christ is the end of the law for righteousness to everyone who believes. Romans 10:3-4*

By Gum

*If then you have been raised with Christ, seek the things
that are above, where Christ is, seated at the right hand of God.
Set your minds on things that are above, not on things
that are on earth. Colossians 3:1-2*

When our daughter was little, she went to great lengths to avoid exposure to chewing gum.

Her paranoia was so fierce that she refused to put her legs under restaurant tables. She somehow managed to square her shoulders with the table, then twist her waist so her legs hung safely at a 90 degree angle off the side of her chair. One time we were at a very fancy restaurant, and my wife assured her there would not be gum under this table. My daughter checked. Apparently sticking one's gum to the bottom of a table is a practice shared by all classes.

Who knows what extremes of ickiness my daughter attached to the substance called gum? I agree that used gum is not appealing and can be a danger when left in walkways, but I never thought twice about whether it might fall off the bottom of a table onto my legs or jump across a room and attack me. Her mind was obsessed, fixated, and set on something irrational but very real to her.

I was reminded of her trauma when I spotted gum on some rocky ground the other day. It was something to be aware of, but not a clear and present danger. In fact its worst threat was taking my eye off of real dangers up above, like a low limb or moving traffic.

Gum seems pretty childish, but life is full of adult obsessions that cause Christ-blindness. Some are about fear (financial security, social identity, the spread of diseases), but Christ rules over all things, including these. Others are about addiction (work as a way of feeling valued, exaggerated identity with a sports team, social media in every spare moment), but Christ is more satisfying than all things, including these.

Life is full of thieves waiting to steal your joy. You have your list of these, and I have mine. But God says there is a better place to set our minds – on Him.

For many years my daughter missed the delight of the food on her plate because she was worried about the gum under the table. One was the reality of a feast, the other was an imagined danger. In Christ, there is a choice.

Today. Right now is a wonderful time to shift your gaze, look Jesus in the eye and fill up on His satisfying grace. Everything else can wait; the feast is before you now.

The Gospel. The devil finds many ways to distract us from God's goodness, none of which satisfies us. But in Jesus we find something different: *"I am the bread of life; whoever comes to Me shall not hunger, and whoever believes in Me shall never thirst." John 6:35* Only in Christ is there satisfaction for the soul – the soul that He created in the first place.

Rules
Rules
Rules

Pickle Perfect
Sorry
Out of Bounds
Keep Out
You Bet

Pickle Perfect

*We remember the fish we ate in Egypt that cost nothing,
the cucumbers, the melons, the leeks, the onions, and the garlic.
But now our strength is dried up, and there is nothing at all
but this manna to look at. Numbers 11:5-6*

We have rules at our house like, "Do not take the plastic play food outside." We also have rule-breakers.

This summer my granddaughter and grandson conspired to pack lunch from the play kitchen for a backyard picnic. They got in a bit of trouble for it. Later I found the chief conspirator poking around in the monkey grass, where he admitted he'd thrown a plastic pickle. The pickle was so lost that he couldn't find it that day, or any other days when he came over.

Fast forward a couple of months, and my family was helping dig weeds out of my flower bed. The next morning I found the pickle tossed up on the patio. My grandson was relieved.

The Israelites were pickle hunters as well. When they were grumbling in the wilderness, they wished they could find some cucumbers like they had in Egypt. You kind of wonder how often they really had those cucumbers in Egypt, but that's another story.

What would they have "found" if they found those cucumbers again? Satisfaction? Refreshment? How about disappointment?

The blessing of the cucumbers was this (and only this): Israel's Sustainer God provided them. As God's redeemed people followed Him away from captivity, they were blind to the new form His blessing was taking. They wanted their security, not His presence. They failed to see that God-empty cucumbers would be of no benefit whatsoever.

I have so many cucumbers in my life – blessings God used to sustain me for a time. They were useful because He was in them, but now He has moved on so I will see my dependence is on Him in whatever form He chooses to take. They might be things like the shape of a family, forms of worship, daily routines, state of health, or a particular job.

Today. Maybe you have some cucumbers, too. What are they? What do you need to let go of, so you can see the new blessings God is inhabiting? He's standing there with new manna in His hands. Take and eat with the thanksgiving He deserves!

The Gospel. *And my God will supply every need of yours according to his riches in glory in Christ Jesus. Philippians 4:19* God's supply may take many forms in this life, tangible signs of His love and care. But His riches are most needed for our souls, which had mistakenly decided they could provide for themselves without Him. Without Him we are lost, and only He can seek us out.

Sorry

In those days there was no king in Israel.
Everyone did what was right in his own eyes. Judges 17:6

Sorry is a board game where you try to move your game pawns from your Start to your Home. The added twist is that you can send other players back to their Start or switch places with them on the board.

I thought I knew how to play Sorry – until my seven-year-old grandson wanted to play it with me. He hauled out a box and set up the pieces. Except each person had three pawns instead of four. And the cards referred to something called Fire and Ice. And the four corner spaces had unfamiliar icons in them.

They changed the rules in 2013! The game I knew no longer existed. In fact, we didn't even know what the new rules were because the instructions were missing from the game box.

It went poorly. Without clear game rules we each "did what was right in our own eyes."

What if real life were like that? What if we all lived without an understanding of the rules?

For many people that's true. They have no instruction sheet except for what seems right to them – as individuals, as communities and as nations. They make up laws, then change them based on popular opinion or their own interests. It goes poorly.

Did you ever stop to consider how merciful God has been to tell us the Rules of Life? He lays out His heart in the Law, wisdom in Proverbs, unmerited provision in the Gospels, and application in the Epistles.

Today. God's rules don't hold believers back. They release us to enjoy the life God created for us. What's your next move?

The Gospel. The mercies of God's grace are boundless. The game Builder told us that Eternal Life is impossible to win in our own strength, then provided us with the Hope that comes from receiving the Victor's pieces as our own. The true King amazingly takes believers from our Start to His Home by entering the world and playing the game perfectly Himself on our behalf.

Out of Bounds

And I will make justice the line,
and righteousness the plumb line. Isaiah 28:17a

In a recent basketball game, one player cleanly snatched the ball from another – but the official blew his whistle anyway. The player's toe barely went over the out-of-bounds line. That's all it took, just the slightest touching of the inside edge of the line.

In other sports it's different.

In soccer the play continues as long as the ball is touching the line, even if the ball is barely touching the outside of the line. The player can be as far out of bounds as she likes, as long as the ball doesn't go past the outside edge of the line.

Question: Which way describes how you think about sin?

Is it the Basketball Way? Do you live your life based on the idea that God has clearly marked the edge of what He is like, and He protects us when He tells us that sin and death lie outside that line?

Or is it the Soccer Way? Do you live your life based on the idea that the inside of the line is only a warning stripe, and it's OK to dart outside when life "requires" it?

Make no mistake: We all step across the line far more than we should. *See Isaiah 53:6.* But what attitude do you have when you do? Do you see life through God's eyes (God's holiness ends where the line begins) or through the world's eyes (the line is a buffer whose width we can define for ourselves)?

Today. How much forgiveness do you think you require? The more clearly you see the line through God's eyes, the more clearly you see how dearly He loved us to *"become [your] sin"* *(see 2 Corinthians 5:21)* and to be judged for your sin *(see Ephesians 5:2)*.

The Gospel. In a game that we had "already lost," God stepped in to snatch away the death we deserved. By grace He did so without breaking a single one of His own righteous boundaries. Perfect love! Perfect justice! He forgave it all – and "all" is way more than we can even imagine.

Keep Out

[God] drove out the man, and at the east of the garden of Eden He placed the cherubim and a flaming sword that turned every way to guard the way to the tree of life. Genesis 3:24

A fence can change a neighborhood overnight – especially if it springs up around a whole section of houses, even blocking off a street. That's what happened to the corner of a busy intersection near our house a few weeks ago. The tall chain link rent-a-fence included prominent signs and yellow caution tape that screamed, "Keep Out or Else!"

Do you sometimes think that's what God's rules are like? "Thou Shalt Not!"

Then I looked closer at the houses. A boarded-up window had another sign: "Danger. Asbestos. Cancer and Lung Disease Hazard."

The ominous fence and signs weren't there to deprive me of liberty. They were there to protect me from danger.

It's the same with God's rules. He may not add signs that identify the dangers that await trespassers, but He knows what is hidden there. His rules are one more expression of His steadfast love!

Do some of God's rules seem unnecessary to you – outdated, bothersome, frustrating? Me, too. But only when I believe Satan's lie that they are keeping me away from things that are good for me. Instead, God has graciously fenced off the things that would steal the joy, providence, life, and blessing He offers.

Today. How do you look at God's rules when you are tempted to trespass one of His instructions – as warning signs, or prison walls? The answer will tell you what you really think about the nature of God and how much He loves you.

The Gospel. *[God] saved us and called us to a holy calling, not because of our works but because of His own purpose and grace, which He gave us in Christ Jesus before the ages began, and which now has been manifested through the appearing of our Savior Christ Jesus, who abolished death and brought life and immortality to light through the Gospel. 2 Timothy 1:9-10*

You Bet

For I am sure that neither death nor life, nor angels nor rulers, nor things present nor things to come, nor powers, nor height nor depth, nor anything else in all creation, will be able to separate us from the love of God in Christ Jesus our Lord. Romans 8:38-39

Are you a gambler?

As a rookie feature writer/illustrator at a small town newspaper, the only people I knew were the other journalists there. Once a week they held a midnight Poker Party. These days I would rather sleep, but back then I took one roll of quarters and just had fun with the gang.

I don't visit casinos or play the lottery anymore. But here's the thing: I still place bets. We all do. We bet our health on what we eat. We bet our schedule on which route we choose. We bet our circumstances on who we trust. We bet our happiness on what we assume.

But here is the biggest bet of all – one where you literally bet every chip you have. "What happens when my physical body dies?"

Some people bet that life on earth is all there is. Some bet that we all pass equally into another life form. Some bet that there is a "good enough" or "tried hard enough" standard they can meet. Some bet on the promise of some other teaching, writing, or philosophy. Some say they are not betting at all.

But you have to bet. There is no sitting out the hand. All chips go on the table, even if they go into a space called "none of the above."

As believers, we have a Helper in the game, the Holy Spirit. By His calling we have been told how the game will end and where to place our bet. While others may fret about their choices, we can play out the game of life with blessed assurance – by God's grace alone. Our treasure is placed well.

Today. It's one thing to bet on your health, schedule, circumstance, or happiness. Those things may seem like your life, but they pale in comparison to victory over death. Delight in the riches that God has laid on the table, and cherish His gift of them to those who heed His call to lay down their lives for Him.

The Gospel. The triune Creator of this world began with a plan, knowing that sin would eternally separate us from His goodness. In the fullness of time He has laid down His cards one by one to reveal the only winning hand in the game – and lovingly invited sinners to repent, fold our own hands, and bet on His hands that were spread out and pierced for our transgressions. Jesus laid down His life that we may be saved.

Faith and
Works

Traditions
Spellbound
Ampersand Religion
The Selfie Survey
Just in Case

Traditions

Remember the Sabbath day, to keep it holy. Exodus 20:8

In the 1960s there was a Carnation ice cream store on the west side of town – a tiny place with vintage metal parlor chairs. For us it was a place of celebration and remembrance.

After the final nervous notes were struck at each year's piano recital, my brother, sister and I knew that the next stop was Carnation! It's what our family did. It was our tradition.

Carnation closed, and I saw Braum's become the new celebration station of choice. Choir concerts, recitals, and history reenactments were often capped by a trip to Braum's. We had two Braum's celebrations recently, a ballet recital and a preschool graduation. It was a bad week for dieting!

It reminds me that God often pointed people to traditions.

He shows us that traditions have power. Through the Passover, God encouraged people to remember Him in a certain way as they crossed through the wilderness.

Traditions also have purpose. God used Passover to foreshadow Christ's purposeful sin-satisfying sacrifice, and His command to commemorate His death and resurrection through the Lord's Supper until His coming again.

And traditions have perpetuity. These traditions point our minds ahead to a time when God has made it possible to celebrate with the Lamb of God face to face – forever!

Be careful what traditions you establish. Jesus cautioned against those who *"leave the commandment of God and hold to the tradition [self-made rules] of men." Mark 7:8*

But be mindful to make traditions as well, of the right kind. Celebrate the good things God gives you to enjoy. Do it with others. Do it with regularity.

Today. What's your plan for Sunday? If one of your traditions is not weekly worship with other Christ followers, you are missing out on something important. Power, purpose, and perpetuity – a foreshadow of an eternity spent in worship of Him. Don't be afraid to be a part of it.

The Gospel. Jesus lived, died, and did something on the third day that was impossible. He stopped being dead. Death could not hold Him because there was no sin to hold Him down. By grace He makes that same righteousness available to everyone who truly believes in Him, and invites His new family to celebrate that fact every Sunday.

Spellbound

What good is it, my brothers, if someone says he has faith but does not have works? Can that faith save him? James 2:14

Do you remember spelling tests? They were pretty boring – except for one. One English teacher at my school always carried a big chip on her shoulder, which made it all the funnier when she called out the word "tarantula."

Instead of saying "tuh-*ran*-chuh-luh" she pronounced it as "ta-ran-*too*-luh." She probably wondered why the whole class snickered and why she became known as Ms. Tarantoola after that.

Let's give this teacher the benefit of the doubt and assume she actually knew what the word meant. Her inability to pronounce it made it a useless part of her vocabulary. Its purpose was unfulfilled.

That reminds me of faith and works.

Knowing the Word = internal faith. It gives hope, motivates us, and is Life to us. It is a blessing beyond imagining that God reveals His Word to us at all, that we should know Him.

Pronouncing the Word correctly = external works. It is speaking the Word into the world and demonstrating that we know Him. It is this sharing that changes the world. The Word's purpose is fulfilled.

Today. Pronouncing is what verifies the knowing. It changes our world inside and out. What are you saying today? Are you pronouncing Jesus' truth?

The Gospel. In the beginning, God spoke what He already knew into existence and tested mankind's trust in Him. Our failure spelled eternal condemnation. But by God's grace, the Word became flesh and called us again to trust in what He did for us. *In the same way, let your light shine before others . . . . Matthew 5:16a*

Ampersand Religion

But when the fullness of time had come,
God sent forth His Son, born of woman, born under the law,
to redeem those who were under the law,
so that we might receive adoption as sons. Galatians 4:4-5

Our three-year-old grandson recently discovered the ampersand (&), and it's now his favorite character to spot and pronounce. Meanwhile, cards and board games have become more popular in the household. That means introducing the concept of "wild cards" – substitutes for other cards you might be needing.

Those two ideas found an unexpected marriage when his six-year-old sister declared a new way to play that car game where you find letters in ABC order as you drive along. You know how hard it is to find letters like Q or Z? Just find ampersands instead. It's the ABC game with wild cards!

Wild cards have their place. But they can also become self-serving & out of place. What if we all started replacing every "and" in our correspondence with &? & what if that included the way we started sentences? & what if we started replacing true faith in Christ with similar shortcuts?

There is no shortage of Ampersand Religion – shortcuts to feeling good about our spiritual condition. Satan loves to see us replacing Christ's lifeblood sacrifice with our own self-justifying works, replacing our share in Christ's afflictions with our own self-appeasing comforts, and replacing Christ's promise of provision with our own expectation of worldly riches.

If shortcuts were possible, God would surely have taken shortcuts Himself. Instead He spent all of history proclaiming His coming, working out our salvation as one "born of woman," and suffering the excruciating curse for our own sins. There was no shortcut possible (e.g., wilderness temptations, Garden of Gethsemane).

Praise God that He gives us a new birth, with new eyes to see through the &s! And that He gives us His Spirit to strengthen us to pass by the &s in favor of His Way, Truth, and Life!

Today. Beware! Satan's temptations are often temptations to shortcuts. & they are lies.

The Gospel. The only Substitute for the death we deserve under our own sin is Christ. By His grace and work we are saved. *And because you are sons, God has sent the Spirit of His Son into our hearts, crying "Abba! Father!" So you are no longer a slave, but a son, and if a son, then an heir through God. Galatians 4:6-7*

The Selfie Survey

You know when I sit down and when I rise up;
you discern my thoughts from afar. Psalm 139:2

For part of my life I was involved with a magazine publishing company where we engaged in survey warfare with our competitors. We would publish a survey that showed how much advertisers preferred our magazine. Competitors would counter with their own self-serving survey. Back and forth we went, year after year.

I wonder how many advertisers realized that publishers sometimes ran several private surveys before we arrived at the one we published. Preliminary surveys helped us craft questions that would give us superior results on the final survey. The results were truthful, but they were truthful responses to selective questions we engineered to present ourselves to advertisers in the best possible light.

Sometimes I am tempted to present myself to God in the same way.

In that case, I take a quick selfie survey using the Ten Commandments. Big fail on this one, not as bad on that one, etc. Then I retake the survey and leave out the questions where I failed. I become convinced that the second survey is who I really am – and that God should see me that way as well.

Two take-aways:

First, I am reminded of something bad. I am not fooling God with my selfie survey. He sees me as I am. *Now it is evident that no one is justified before God by the law. Galatians 3:11*

Second, I am reminded of something good. God has thrown out my pseudo-survey and substituted the result of Christ's life, which perfectly satisfies the law on my behalf. *We also have believed in Christ Jesus, in order to be justified by faith in Christ. Galatians 2:16*

The first take-away reminds us that we have much work to do. The second take-away reminds us it is not we who do this work, but Christ.

Today. Rejoice in this: When God presents you with a survey form asking which commandments you have kept, you will not have to check "None of the Above." Instead you can check "Accomplished by the One Above." Amen and amen.

The Gospel. *There is therefore now no condemnation for those who are in Christ Jesus. For the law of the Spirit of life has set you free in Christ Jesus from the law of sin and death. Romans 8:1-2*

Just in Case

*Behold, God is my salvation; I will trust,
and will not be afraid. Isaiah 12:2a*

The young woman at our restaurant table had a story, and I'm still not sure how much was fact and fiction. Danielle had stopped us on the sidewalk looking for a hot meal. She accepted our invitation to join us for lunch and gladly ordered on our tab.

She said her boyfriend had booted her out of his life, and she'd been pounding the pavement looking for a job. The conversation turned to trust. "I've learned that the only person you can trust is yourself," she declared.

"You know," I said, "you can't trust yourself, either! The Bible has story after story about people who tried to trust themselves. And I know from my own experience why they always failed. I make promises to myself that I fail to keep all the time! Why am I drinking this sweet tea right now, when I told myself I would start drinking more water?"

Then we went briefly through the Good News that God spends all of human history foretelling . . . then living as a man . . . then dying for our sins (our ongoing efforts to trust ourselves instead of Him) . . . then proving His power over death with resurrection. I felt like she was letting me tell a story she'd heard a million times before, the cost of accepting a meal from a stranger. But you never know.

She may not have been convicted right then of her misplaced trust, but God was telling me plenty about my own. I kept second-guessing, "Am I telling this story well enough?"

I realized I was falling into that same old trap – wanting to trust myself with the story instead of trusting God to use whatever words He laid on my heart at the moment. What a paradox. What a reminder that my ongoing need for Jesus' grace never ends.

Today. Who are you counting on today – God or Self? Or maybe that question is too simple. While you count on God, are you still holding onto some expectations of your Self to pull out "just in case?" So am I. But God is working on that. He's already prepared the feast and paid the tab. May His story fall on fresh ears every day, and especially mine (and yours).

The Gospel. *Such is the confidence that we have through Christ toward God. Not that we are sufficient in ourselves to claim anything as coming from us, but our sufficiency is from God. 2 Corinthians 3:4-5*

Marvelous Me

Me, Myself, I
My Majesty
Mine!
The No-Snow Snowman

Me, Myself, I

And [you] have put on the new self, which is being renewed
in knowledge after the image [identity] of its Creator. Colossians 3:10

That's Batman in the picture. Or is it our grandson? In his
mind there is no difference.

Who are you today? Take a look at the decal on your truck, the label on your jeans, the insignia on your shirt, or the diploma on your wall.

We all yearn to be identified with something bigger than ourselves. We want to be acknowledged, appreciated, and associated.

Remember Woody in the movie *Toy Story*? At some point, when Woody is feeling like his boy Andy doesn't care about him anymore, he discovers something written on the bottom of one of his boots – the word "Andy."

Andy had identified Woody as his own, and that gave Woody the assurance he needed that Andy loved him.

Somebody has written His name on you! He is ultimately all the identity you need. He is the only identity worth trusting. Those other identities? God calls them "idols."

By grace, Jesus chooses to identify some people as His own, and makes us to identify with Him. His strength in us is beyond our imagining.

Today. It's okay to have interests in the world, but don't let them become idols. There's only one identity worth having – the one written on your heart. Everything else? Let's just say that wearing Batman pajamas doesn't make us Batman. There's only room for one superhero in heaven, and He's already there.

The Gospel. Christ came that sinners' names might be written in the Book of Life with His blood. *And you show that you are a letter from Christ delivered by us, written not with ink but with the Spirit of the living God, not on tablets of stone but on tablets of human hearts. 2 Corinthians 3:3*

My Majesty

To the King of the ages, immortal, invisible, the only God,
be honor and glory forever and ever. Amen. 1 Timothy 1:17

My granddaughter and I were driving to church one day when she mysteriously said, "Pop, I think you need a new name."

I joked, "How about 'Your Majesty'?"

"No," she said. "I already chose that name for myself."

And it struck me how all of us are just like that.

God says, "I want to call you by a new name," meaning a name like Redeemed. And we reply, "No, I already have a name picked out, Mr. God. How about You call me Your Majesty?"

That's when He has to correct us and explain that only He is majesty. We get it all backwards. We tell God, "I am adorable," when we should be screaming, "Only You are worthy of adoration!"

Soon thereafter, I ran across this marvelous quote:

"We have turned everyone to his own way" (Isaiah 53:6) describes the course which we all follow by nature. Before conversion every soul lives to please self. Of old it was written, "every man did that which was right in his own eyes," and why? "In those days there was no King in Israel" (Judges 21:25). Ah! that is the point we desire to make clear to the reader. Until Christ becomes your King (1 Timothy 1:17; Revelation 15:3), until you bow to His scepter, until His will becomes the rule of your life, self dominates, and thus Christ is disowned.
– Arthur Pink in *Is Christ Your Lord*?

Today. Who is your Holy today? Which way do you bow?

The Gospel. There is only one throne in heaven, occupied by Jesus. This same Jesus surrendered His body to crucifixion, then rose in victory over death, that we might come to worship His majesty forever. *After this I heard what seemed to be the loud voice of a great multitude in heaven, crying out, "Hallelujah! Salvation and glory and power belong to our God...." Revelation 19:1*

Mine!

Whoever has two tunics is to share with him who has none, and whoever has food is to do likewise. Luke 3:11

When our granddaughter goes to church with us, we bring things like books, coloring pages and a snack to keep her busy during the service.

On this particular day we had pulled out her Cheez-Its and opened the container. I asked if she wanted to share some with her friend in the pew. Her response? She fiercely crammed them tightly against her side to hide them from her friend. It was obvious she wanted every last bite for herself.

"How selfish!" I thought. And right here in church, of all places! But I had to reconsider my judgmental attitude when I realized how much I am like that, too. "This is my pew.... I was going to talk to that guy after church when somebody else butted in. My friend.... I love that song, but only played my way."

It's the same outside of church. "My life is mine.... That parking space is mine.... That time slot is mine.... That job security is mine."

Then Jesus reminds me: *Whoever finds his life will lose it, and whoever loses his life for my sake will find it. Matthew 10:39* I can settle for my own life, but His life is far superior. While I am desperately holding onto my Cheez-Its, Jesus is offering me a feast beyond my imagining right now.

Today. Which "mine" is ruling what you think, say, and do today? Are you willing to adopt the humility of Christ and surrender it to Him – and even share it with someone else around you?

The Gospel. When Jesus felt the rightful punishment of your sins on the cross, He was able to say, "It is finished. You are now mine." He is our only Mine – our supreme Treasure. Never let Him go!

The No-Snow Snowman

Therefore, if anyone is in Christ, he is a new creation.
the old has passed away;
behold, the new has come. 2 Corinthians 5:17

Snow! Snow! Snow! I was so excited that the meteorologist said some of the little ones around our house might get to build a snowman in Texas. Snow is mesmerizing in our culture, and snowmen are magical. Why else would my head still be throbbing with the songs from *Frozen*? Maybe the snow would give kids a better chance at building their own Olaf.

But the snow was a bit of a letdown in our neighborhood. Not enough to cover the grass, much less make a snowman. And more like ice than snow. So I took matters into my own hands.

I got out three Cocoa Puffs and three grape tomatoes. I

manufactured my own traditional snowman shapes. I planted them in the flowerbed's crust of sleet.

Frankly, the results were not the same as building a real snowman. By changing the composition of the material, there was something missing – the snow!

Sometimes I'm tempted to build my life like those pseudo-snowmen. I reach back into the pantry of my worldly strengths. I puff out my chest and emulate a shape. I present myself to the world. And I fail. From the perspective of holiness and majestic beauty, I look like Cocoa Puffs and grape tomatoes in a field of snow.

That's why I am so very grateful that God does not see me that way in Christ. He sees me as His finished work, a spectacular sculpture packed to just the right density and shaped to perfection. On the surface I shimmer in His light and – most important of all – I am of His essence to the very core.

The transformation is still in progress, but it is assured. Praise God, whose image we bear in Christ!

Today. What are you made of? Is your substance becoming more like Christ all the time, as His life is shaping yours? Or is it a counterfeit destined to disintegrate or shrivel away? Salvation belongs to the Lord, who knows all forecasts from the beginning.

The Gospel. *And we all, with unveiled face, beholding the glory of the Lord, are being transformed into the same image from one degree of glory to another. For this comes from the Lord who is the Spirit. 2 Corinthians 3:18*

A Joyful Noise

Audio Deo
The Winning Laugh
Awake!
Commencement
Bride of Christ

Audio Deo

For it is not you who speak, but the Spirit of your Father
speaking through you. Matthew 10:20

Our grandson brought some play "microphones" to a family gathering last month. A few days later his cousin asked, "How does a microphone make you sound louder?" I wasn't quite sure how to answer a five-year-old on that one, since I try to avoid using the internet while driving. "Well, it picks up your voice and sends it to something called an amplifier, which . . . ." I had already lost her, but it did remind me how God helps us glimpse spiritual truths by considering His physical creation.

God gives the world a message, the Gospel. He adds His voice, the Word that we did not have before. He provides an amplifier, the Holy Spirit. Then He seeks out speakers, those who are redeemed and reborn.

Sometimes His Spirit makes the voice speak boldly and directly and loudly and publicly. Sometimes He makes it speak softly and sacrificially and privately. Sometimes He prepares that voice through formal training. Sometimes He prepares that voice through hard times and necessity.

His voice is always prepared in just the right way for just the right circumstance, and it is always amplified to just the right people at just the right time. By God's grace, it can even speak through you today.

Today. *Make a joyful noise to the LORD, all the earth; break forth into joyous song and sing praises! Psalm 98:4*

The Gospel. The Voice that spoke all things into existence became flesh-existent, that we might hear of His grace and experience His mercy.

The Winning Laugh

Jesus . . . who for the joy that was set before Him endured the cross. Hebrews 12:2

Many years ago at a lake resort in Arkansas we attended

our first Family Camp. Our church hosted the week-long event, including numerous organized and free-form activities, skits, worship, and more.

It was a week of firsts. I broke my first bone. I overturned my first jet ski and trapped my wife underwater. And my son won the contest for "Most Sincere Laugh" (as gauged by audience applause)!

I thought of that award the other day when my granddaughter announced that she had many different voices – including her "fake" and "real" laughs.

What is the measure of a "real" laugh? How did Jesus laugh? I think we find it in *1 Peter 1:8-9. Though you have not seen Him, you love Him. Though you do not now see Him, you believe in Him and rejoice with joy that is inexpressible and filled with glory, obtaining the outcome of your faith, the salvation of your souls.*

Jesus has joy that overflows because it is beyond human expression and filled with glory. What a laugh that must be – a victory laugh to beat all victory laughs! It's joy that He delivered a call to repentance, joy that His life made forgiveness possible, and joy that His sheep are redeemed to spend eternity living out the worshipful purpose for which they were made.

The "Most Sincere Laugh" award really belongs to Jesus. But when He lives in your heart He gives you that same laugh of joy as you behold His glory.

Today. Jesus is the object of your worship and you are the object of His affection. Forget the "fake laugh." You have the real thing.

The Gospel. By submitting Himself to the most grievous

and tragic atrocities of man, the Man of Sorrows rose to laugh at a grave that could not hold Him. He made it possible for us to believe in Him and rejoice as He obtained the outcome of our God-given faith, the salvation of our souls.

Awake!

At the Transfiguration:
Now Peter and those who were with him were heavy with sleep, but when they became fully awake they saw [Jesus'] glory and the two men [Moses and Elijah] who stood with Him. Luke 9:32

When our granddaughter spends a Saturday night with us, she sleeps like a rock. The best way to get her up in time for worship on Sunday is to turn on the TV, which wakes up her awareness. Then we ask her which breakfast food she wants, which wakes up her anticipation. Then we wiggle the bed, which wakes up her motion.

In a few minutes she stirs – then she suddenly becomes fully awake as the reality of a new day dawns!

Our heavenly Father does the same thing for us. We are deep asleep in our sins and our preoccupation with the world. But He has prepared a New Day for those He awakens. In His loving mercy He wakes up our awareness of our need for Him. Then He wakes up our anticipation of New Life in Him. Then He wakes up our motion to live out this New Life.

He turns our deep sleep into fully-awakeness!

Peter, James and John had no idea what would happen when they accompanied Jesus up a mountain one day. They were tired and groggy and immersed in this world. But Jesus knew He was leading them to see Him in His glory!

Today. Me too! Me too! Now that you're awake, do you want to see more of the astounding Christ who awoke you?

The Gospel.
Love not sleep [and dreams of worldly things],
Lest you come to poverty [a life whose rewards are
in this world];
Open your eyes [be born again in Christ],
and you will have plenty of bread [salvation forevermore].
Proverbs 20:13

Commencement

*Now to Him who is able to keep you from stumbling
and to present you blameless before the presence of His glory
with great joy, to the only God, our Savior, through Jesus Christ
our Lord, be glory, majesty, dominion, and authority, before
all time and now and forever. Amen. Jude 1:24-25*

As spring gives way to summer, social media once again lights up with posts about the pros and cons of preschool graduation ceremonies. I attended one of those graduations myself a few weeks ago.

The cons usually get the ball rolling, lamenting the practice of caps and gowns for kids who have done little more than show up for learning-by-play. Let's not diminish the celebration of real achievement later by role-playing today, they say. The pros respond, poo-pooing the idea that this is not about what kids have achieved. Let's celebrate the little folks' passage from one growth stage to the next, they say. Who cares if they wear caps and gowns? They love dress-up.

I'm not taking sides on this one, at least not here. But it

does make me think about the day when we will graduate from this earthly life into Jesus' glorious presence.

I noticed a few things at preschool graduation.

First, our own kid got our best applause, because we're family. God's delight in the work He has done in us will also be whole-hearted joy when we are glorified with Christ – because He adopted us as His children. *See Matthew 12:18.*

Next, the kids were all dressed the same. Their caps and gowns marked them as graduates, but they were still individual and identifiable. Soon God will dress us individually in His uniform robe of righteousness, the mark of His eternal blessing. *See 2 Timothy 4:8.*

Finally, they were still kids, not all that smart or experienced. We may think much of ourselves, but we will suddenly find out how far short of God's glory we are, even at our best, when we see Him face to face! *See Romans 3:23.* The best is yet to come, when He makes us complete!

One name that God uses for Christ-followers is "disciples" – not the type of student who studies to pass a course, but one who studies the Object of her affection because she simply cannot get enough of Him.

As you grapple with the often-painful course of study God has set you on during this life, remember that suddenly (in the twinkling of an eye) you will be graduated, and face-to-face life with Jesus will commence! There you will be, spending an eternity at the feet of Jesus Himself, the good Teacher.

Today. Enjoy your preschool years. But the best is yet to come.

The Gospel. Only if your transcript includes Christ's

righteousness can you be accepted into His eternal discipleship, and that righteousness is a free gift. To those who have that gift, *The Spirit and the Bride say, "Come." And let the one who hears say, "Come." And let the one who is thirsty come; let the one who desires take the water of life without price. Revelation 22:17*

Bride of Christ

"Come, I will show you the Bride, the wife of the Lamb."
Revelation 21:9b

My daughter looked radiant in her wedding gown. Her heart was beating furiously. So nervous. So full of joyful anticipation. So anxious about the unknown. My heart matched hers, as we stood arm-in-arm in the foyer of the church, staring at the double doors that would open in just . . .

5 seconds. How did 25 years pass so quickly?

4 seconds. I remembered her in pink footy pajamas.

3 seconds. I remembered her at camp.

2 seconds. I remembered our date nights.

1 second. I remembered her moving out and getting her first job.

Now!

The doors swung open, and every eye in the church turned toward us. The bride stepped forward, "entering God's gate with thanksgiving, His courts with praise." In just a few moments, I presented her to her groom, with whom she will spend the rest of her life.

Even then, it reminded me that each believer in Christ is standing right where my daughter and I stood last week. We are in the foyer of this life, walking arm in arm with God. At any moment, He may cause the doors to swing open that lead us into the perfect heavenly presence of Christ – who is our bridegroom!

I wonder . . .

Does my heart beat as furiously for that heavenly moment as it did in the foyer that day?

Am I as full of joyful anticipation for the moment when God will escort me from this life into the life that weds us?

Am I remembering that the moment will be just as real (only more so) as the rush my daughter and I felt when those doors were flung open for her?

Today. The bridegroom awaits more eagerly than you can imagine. Are your longing and anticipation growing just as eagerly, befitting a bride whose bridegroom stands just one door away?

The Gospel. God is not a distant, uncaring ruler over mankind, but a steadfast Savior who seeks out and rescues those on whom He has set His affections for all time. *And if I go and prepare a place for you, I will come again and will take you to Myself, that where I am you may be also. And you know the way to where I am going. John 14:3-4*

Road Trip

Same Day Delivery
The Chevy Chase
The Long Haul
What a Bother

Same Day Delivery

This is the day that the Lord has made.
Let us rejoice and be glad in it! Psalm 118:24

I saw this truck on the road the other day. By replacing one letter with another, the company was pointing out its value proposition: "Someday vs. Same Day. Same Day is better."

The Bible is full of stories about people who yearned for Same Day delivery. God's people cried out for deliverance from slavery, attackers, heartache, and guilt under the law – now! They watched anxiously on their front porches for the arrival of a promised Redeemer – now!

Then one day, in the City of David, a child was born who was Christ the Lord. In God's perfect timing, the Deliverer came to share in flesh and blood. By His work and proclamation, He spoke words of forgiveness and relieved individuals of their most urgent and enduring burden, their sin – immediately, Same Day. For example: *"But that you may know that the Son of Man has authority on earth to forgive sins," [Jesus] said to the paralytic, "I say to you, rise, pick up your bed, and go home." And he rose and immediately picked up his bed and went out. Mark 2:10-12*

I wonder how that paralytic's life changed that day. I wonder what message gripped his heart each morning. I wonder what hope drove his words and actions. I wonder how people saw the difference in him.

I have to ask those same things about myself. I have already been delivered forever from the sins I have loved and death I have deserved. So what's different about my affections, thoughts and actions today? Do people see the difference in me?

Yes, there is still more to come. "Someday" is still on God's delivery truck. He sets that Someday before us as an encouragement to strengthen us under this world's duress. But the essence of God's free and precious gift is already yours! You are set free to come into the presence of holy God, as a beloved child. His blood has opened the way. His affections are set upon you, and He delights in your desire for Him.

Today. God's mercies are new every morning. *See Lamentations 3:23.* What are you doing with your Same Day delivery of His grace today?

The Gospel. We have been delivered! *And you, who were dead in your trespasses and the uncircumcision of your flesh, God made alive together with Him, having forgiven us all our trespasses, by canceling the record of debt that stood against us*

with its legal demands. This He set aside, nailing it to the cross.
Colossians 2:13

The Chevy Chase

Whatever is true, honorable, just, pure, lovely, commendable –
if there is any excellence, anything worthy of praise –
think about these things. Philippians 4:8

"There's a Chevy!" ... "That's a Toyota!" ... "There's another Toyota!"

My six-year-old granddaughter has noticed that vehicles have logos and names. Last week our drive was punctuated by her various identifications. I'm not sure why car-spotting has become her new sport, but it might be because her parents have been car shopping.

Maybe you've shopped for cars, too. While you once drove along oblivious to other vehicles, you suddenly become hyper-alert to every car in sight – especially your dream car. You might even speed up to chase down a car you wanted to see more closely. At least that's my experience.

Your interest is always tuned to what your heart desires!

Think of a time when your mind was bent on doing something you knew would dishonor God. On another day you might have ignored the whisper to "do that," but on that day your spiritual ears were tuned to that temptation's frequency. Everything you passed reminded you to want (need, deserve) "that."

Did you speed up to chase down that evil for a closer look? That's the broken human nature we still live with. We are hardwired from birth to chase evil. Then we find out how unsatisfying it is when we catch it. Without Christ that is our lot, now and forever.

No wonder the Bible is filled with desperate people yearning for a "Redeemer," one who could break the cycle and save them from themselves!

Today we have that Redeemer, Jesus Christ. He lived the only unsinning life in history. Then He spent that life to present Himself as a sacrifice, to satisfy the eternal consequence of sins we could never take back. Because He did, our desires can be fixed on better things. For those who are in Christ, the Holy Spirit enables you to dwell on what is "worthy of praise" – the result of loving Him with all your heart.

Today. What are you thinking about today? At this moment? Is it worthy of the new logo and name that Jesus put on you?

The Gospel. *And such were some of you. But you were washed, you were sanctified, you were justified in the name of the Lord Jesus Christ and by the Spirit of our God. 1 Corinthians 6:11*

The Long Haul

Five times I received at the hands of the Jews the forty lashes less one. Three times I was beaten with rods. Once I was stoned. Three times I was shipwrecked; a night and a day I was adrift at sea; on frequent journeys, in danger from rivers, danger from robbers, danger from my own people, danger from Gentiles, danger in the city, danger in the wilderness, danger at sea, danger from false brothers; in toil and hardship, through many a sleepless night, in hunger and thirst, often without food, in cold and exposure. 2 Corinthians 11: 24-27

Driving down the street the other day, I came alongside a work truck. Prominent in the back was a yellow wheelbarrow – a wheelbarrow riddled with pock marks, dings, dents and other signs of rigorous use. Can you imagine the stories written on those bumpy sides? Countless loads of construction material, beating down its fresh paint and smooth surfaces. Shovels striking with total disregard for its condition or feelings.

A wheelbarrow is built to haul, which has inherent hazards. It leaves the warehouse to fulfill a purpose – and becomes battered in the process.

You and I have an intended use, as well. We read where Paul was willing to live out his purpose in spite of the inherent hazards that lay ahead. His life was spent on hauling God's Good News to a world whose builders reveled in rejecting its chief Cornerstone.

At God's direction, Noah built a wooden boat while the world mocked; in it he hauled his family and animals to a new land. The Israelites built a wooden box while the world ignored; in it they hauled the law of blessing and cursing to a new land. The Romans built a wooden cross while the world cheered; on it Jesus hauled His chosen people to a new hope – taking all our sin onto Himself so that God's wrath fell squarely on Him.

What is God building through you? What is His intended use? Are you surprised to find your smooth surfaces dented, your fresh paint scraped, and your load heavy? Don't be. God is displaying Himself through you, not as a museum piece but as a tool. You are participating in His workmanship.

Today. Just as Paul's purposeful, passionate endurance was an encouragement to the church of his day, your God-enabled endurance brings encouragement to other believers now. Hang in there. Keep going. Christians are in it for the long haul. And when you think about an eternity with Christ, the long haul is Good News indeed! *Therefore encourage one another and build one another up, just as you are doing. 1 Thessalonians 5:11*

The Gospel. *Surely [Christ] has borne our griefs and carried our sorrows; yet we esteemed Him stricken, smitten by God, and afflicted. But He was pierced for our transgressions; He was crushed for our iniquities; upon Him was the chastisement that brought us peace, and with His wounds we are healed. Isaiah 53:4-5*

What a Bother

*"Which of these three, do you think, proved to be
a neighbor to the man who fell among robbers?"
[The lawyer] said, "The one who showed him mercy."
And Jesus said, "You go, and do likewise." Luke 10:36-37*

6:00 p.m. – I expected a quick trip home on the highway after an errand. Suddenly red lights lit up across four lanes and traffic came to a dead stop. Ahead was a wreck that blocked all lanes but one. I finally worked my way through. What a bother.

6:00 a.m. – The next morning I expected a clear highway to work, but found instead a wreck that shut down the highway ahead of me. I finally got to an exit ramp and – accompanied by a stunning number of early risers – worked my way around the wreck. What a bother.

Two accidents within 12 hours of each other. Multiple vehicles crushed and parts strewn across the oily roadway. Shaken drivers and passengers huddled in the dark. So many plans put on hold.

All that, and my best thought was "What a bother"? Shame on me. I spent inconvenient minutes on the scene and went my merry way. Those involved spent miserable hours there plus more time dealing with the aftermath.

I bet you ran into a wreck today – the kind that doesn't happen on highways. Somebody in your life may be shaken by a circumstance, huddled in a dark place, or picking up a broken life.

What was your response? What a bother, or What an opportunity?

Jesus' parable of the Good Samaritan gives us an instruction in how to love each other – without partiality or regard for our own security and comfort. And that is the story of how He loved us, passing from the holy side of the roadway to touch and tend to the filth of our sin.

It was a bother, but that's the point.

Today. Love is a bother. Who have you been bothered by today?

The Gospel. Every person is a wreck who God could rightly pass by. But He bothered with us. *For by grace you have been saved through faith. And this is not your own doing; it is the gift of God, not a result of works, so that no one may boast. For we are His workmanship, created in Christ Jesus for good works, which God prepared beforehand, that we should walk in them. Ephesians 2:8-10*

Holidays

He is Missing
Parade
Foot Work
A Halloween Carol
Face to Face
Expectations

Easter
He is Missing

*They have taken the Lord out of the tomb, and we do not know
where they have laid Him. John 20:2b*

When is the last time you lost something dear to you? Several years ago I came home and emptied my pockets. The next morning I could not find my car key. I've turned the house upside down to no avail. I'm still driving with the spare key today.

When our granddaughter was four, the TV reported that a boy was missing. She wanted to help so she created a sign: "Can you find [picture of boy]. He's missing." We dutifully taped it to our front door.

I've always thought of that sign at Easter. What panic must have ensued for Jesus' followers when their Lord was suddenly snatched from His earthly life. How much more so when He went missing from the tomb! "Can you find Him? Can you? Can you?" We may read right past that moment in the Gospels now, and forget the intense angst that must have washed over them.

Jesus was out of their sight. He was beyond their reach.

Then He showed Himself to them again – to Mary Magdalene and the disciples (*see John 20*), and to many hundreds more *(see 1 Corinthians 15)*. What rejoicing there must have been!

Easter is a good time to remember that something critical was missing from your life – out of your sinful sight, beyond your reach. By grace, God showed Himself to you. More than that, He made it possible for you to be His child instead of His enemy.

Today. Rejoice because He is found! He is Risen! He is Risen indeed!

The Gospel. *I am the resurrection and the life. Whoever believes in Me, though he die, yet shall he live, and everyone who lives and believes in Me shall never die. John 11:25-26*

Independence Day
Parade!

Your procession is seen, O God, the procession of my God, my King, into the sanctuary. Psalm 68:24

"Look! The fire truck is moving!"

We love watching the local neighborhood parade because it is up close and personal. From our position we could see the vehicles forming up and the fire truck announcing the start with a siren. The July 4th parade was under way!

Parades are designed to mark all sorts of grandiose occasions, not just Independence Day. They conjure up images of people celebrating in the streets,

Parades celebrate conquering heroes, past triumphs and future hopes. Long before cities feted Super Bowl champions and Macy's launched a Thanksgiving Day parade, King David led a parade to bring the Ark back to Jerusalem after the Philistines had captured it. A rejoicing crowd turned Jesus' entry into Jerusalem into a parade route, laying down palm branches. A crowd later paraded Jesus through Jerusalem's streets, laying down His blood even before He reached the cross.

Like that crowd, we may be tempted to join a parade just because it's a parade. Our culture is full of people charging en masse toward ungodly heroes, transitory triumphs and misspent hopes. But God's ways are not their ways. God's ways are far more glorious and everlasting. His parade is far closer and more intimate.

"Look! God is moving!" we can see and say. He makes Himself known, with special eyes that He has given to those who have seen their own sin and run to Him as their only hope. The Good Shepherd draws us close enough that we can see and feel and touch Him with our hearts.

Every parade route comes to an end, when the bands disperse and the vehicles are stripped of their finery – every parade except the one that follows the Lord. That parade celebrates forever.

Today. Rejoice that God draws you to His parade, and pray that you may walk diligently as one who is captivated by His triumphant salvation. And remember, sometimes that parade leads to the cross. Thank God He went there before us.

The Gospel. *But thanks be to God, who in Christ always leads us in triumphal procession, and through us spreads the fragrance of the knowledge of Him everywhere. 2 Corinthians 2:14*

Labor Day
Foot Work

[The Lord] drew me up from the pit of destruction,
out of the miry bog, and set my feet upon a rock,
making my steps secure. Psalm 40:2

I celebrated Labor Day wearing feet that didn't match. One had swelled to immense proportions.

At first the doctor suspected gout. Two medicines and a few weeks later, he wasn't so sure. After two more antibiotics, two X-rays, an MRI, a nuclear bone scan, and a specialist, the diagnosis shifted to a foot bone infection. Now I'm feeding daily doses of a menacing antibiotic through a 40mm tube, planted in the arm, that terminates someplace inside my chest – right above the heart, in fact.

It seems odd: To treat the foot infection, you go through the heart. What a marvelous reminder of the paradoxical way that God brings life to a terminally ill world.

Forget about my foot for a minute. Think instead about something far more substantial that has crippled you, me, and every person born – the infection of sin that hides even deeper than a bone infection. It is impossible to root out and cure. It is an irreversible death sentence, worse than anything like cancer. It touches every member of our bodies, every thought in our minds, and every intention, motive and purpose.

Good news: God successfully treats that killer infection (but only through the heart).

Christ the High Priest poured out His own heart-blood so you might live. You are cured. The infection is eliminated, because Christ has made your heart new. *And I will give you a new heart, and a new spirit I will put within you. And I will remove the heart of stone from your flesh and give you a heart of flesh. Ezekiel 36:26*

Today. That news makes my heart soar more than healing a bone infection ever could – but only when I remember it. Are you remembering it today? Are you counting on it, and storing it up in your heart, and letting it set your feet on the Rock? If you knew everything about everything, it's the one thing you would have wished for. And it's yours, believer. That's worth an Amen.

The Gospel. *Let us draw near with a true heart in full assurance of faith, with our hearts sprinkled clean from an evil conscience and our bodies washed with pure water. Hebrews 10:22*

Halloween
A Halloween Carol

Do not neglect to show hospitality to strangers, for thereby some have entertained angels unawares. Hebrews 13:2

It's a bright November morning, the first Sunday after the holiday the world calls "Halloween." Our five-year-old granddaughter and I are making a quick trip through the convenience store near church and heading for the checkout.

"Hi, sweetheart," says Carol the cashier. "Did you get plenty of candy for Halloween?" "Not really," says my little girl, whose definition of Plenty is pretty extravagant.

"Oh dear!" exclaims Carol. "I have so much leftover candy at my house! If you come back tomorrow I will bring you a whole bag!"

Well, granddaughter and Carol were both so excited I could hardly say No. But it's not close to our house and I neglected to make it back the next day. I tried to call a few times, but failed to catch Carol. I was glad to find her there when I was back in the neighborhood the following Saturday. I asked her about it, and guess what? "I brought in the candy Tuesday, and somebody took it from under the counter. But will the little girl be here tomorrow? I still want to give her something." "Oh, please don't feel obligated," I said. But she insisted.

My granddaughter was excited to find out we were going back to the store, and sure enough Carol had a big bag of sweets for her. Both were beaming with the joy of giving and receiving! But Carol beamed more. The Bible clearly states, *"It is more blessed to give than to receive." Acts 20:35* There is a joy in cheerful giving.

Perhaps that's why James said to "count it all joy" when you face trials of self-sacrifice. *See James 1:2.* And why Jesus *"for the joy that was set before Him endured the cross." See Hebrews 12:2.*

That's the point. Not that you should emulate a generous woman, but that you should treasure the ultimate gift of Christ. Jesus gave more than you and I will ever have to give. He gave up heaven to give Himself for you, so the Father might forgive you and give you eternal holy life.

Even our best gift-giving is easily marred by lingering hints of self-importance, expecting recognition, or feeling good about ourselves. But Jesus' sin-bearing, life-purifying gift of Himself was unblemished in its motivation – to exalt the Highest Being out of pure and supreme love.

Today. In the classic story *A Christmas Carol*, the ghosts of past, present and future unfold the difference that one man makes. From the Bible we know that the ultimate difference-maker for all future times is this Man, Jesus Christ. Let us come to Him like little children to receive and adore Him!

The Gospel. *But God, being rich in mercy, because of the great love with which He loved us, even when we were dead in our trespasses, made us alive together with Christ – by grace you have been saved – and raised us up with Him and seated us with Him in the heavenly places in Christ Jesus, so that in the coming ages He might show the immeasurable riches of His grace in kindness toward us in Christ Jesus. For by grace you have been saved through faith. And this is not your own doing; it is the gift of God. Ephesians 2:4-8*

Advent and Christmas
Face to Face

For now we see in a mirror dimly, but then face to face.
Now I know in part; then I shall know fully,
even as I have been fully known. 1 Corinthians 13:12

Like it or not, the winter holiday season has been in full swing since mid-October at area retailers. The centerpiece of the production, Christmas, is a magical time – larger than life!

Several years ago, we watched children at a Christmas

program behold the arrival of St. Nicholas. That's our grandson on the left side of the picture. His eyes are fixed in wonder, his hand poised to either reach out and touch or shield him from the jolly fellow's overwhelming presence. Behind him is our granddaughter, both hiding behind her cousin and unable to tear her eyes away.

The other children's expressions were just as revealing. Joyful. Dazed. Expectant. Puzzled. Awestruck. They've heard the stories. They've seen the pictures. And now he's here!

This picture always makes me wonder what our faces will be like when we see the glorified Christ face to face for the very first time. He is the most wondrous thing our eyes will ever see. He is the most wondrous sound our ears will ever hear. He is too wondrous to comprehend – or ignore.

Today. You've read the Book. You've heard the stories. You've experienced the life-changing Spirit. And now – during the season of Advent that leads up to Christmas – it's time to consider the reality of His appearance. He's here! Can you even begin to imagine how you (as a believer who has placed your life in His hands) will respond when you see Jesus face to face?

The Gospel. Jesus stands ready to save those who cannot save themselves, from an eternal curse and the consequences of their sin. *But Jesus said, "Let the little children come to Me and do not hinder them, for to such belongs the kingdom of heaven." Matthew 19:14*

New Year's Eve

Expectations

Therefore do not be anxious about tomorrow,
for tomorrow will be anxious for itself.
Sufficient for the day is its own trouble. Matthew 6:34

As each new year approaches, I turn the page in my Day-Timer to find an insert with this reminder: "Order Next Year's Day-Timer Dated Planner NOW!" If you want a smooth Day-Timer transition into next year, you'd better act today! That raises some interesting questions about expectations. Would you order a new Day-Timer if you did not believe that time will continue to exist? That the physical world will continue to exist? That you will continue to exist? That you will continue to exist for a purpose that needs this Day-Timer, such as having the same job? That you will continue to be able to exist for this purpose, based on your health or other circumstances?

Expectations about time-events are called assumptions. Expectations about the timeless Creator-Redeemer are called faith. It's easy to get the two confused, but there is a world of difference:

Assumptions consider what might be. Faith considers what will always be.

Assumptions consider what might be lost. Faith considers what cannot be lost.

Assumptions consider my walk through creation. Faith considers the Creator's walk through me.

In the end, I will probably order a new Day-Timer – not because I assume in the days to come, but because I have faith in the Christ who tends the days. Because He lives in each one of them, you and I can turn the page with eager anticipation of what He has prepared for us.

Today. Calendars help us look forward to what we intend to do – to plan in ways that make the best use of our time and prioritize the most important appointments. What's on your schedule for tomorrow? Do any of your appointments include some moments with God, whose heavens are the cornerstone on which your calendar is built?

The Gospel. *I thank You that You have answered me and have become my salvation. The stone that the builders rejected has become the cornerstone. This is the LORD's doing; it is marvelous in our eyes. This is the day that the LORD has made; let us rejoice and be glad in it. Psalm 118:21-24*

Getting
Personal

Monday on the Merry Go Round
Sweet Jeans
Groovy Buttons
Bounce
Gi Whiz

Monday on the Merry Go Round

Thoughts on layoffs and other sudden changes in life

Here we are – another day on the merry go round, perched on our life-sized carousel animals to do our jobs. Remember when the ride opened? The adventurous riders raced to the animals that bob up and down. The more conservative people

settled for the animals on stationary poles. Then there are the
real fuddy-duddies who found the one wagon or sleigh on the
carousel and plopped down on the safe seats. But we all have
this in common: We are on the ride.

By merry go round I mean a painted wood base and
something representing a tent with a pennant on the top.
Bright flashing lights. Blaring music. And a stampede of shiny,
slick horses so big that they could easily crush you under their
hefty hooves as the whole contraption whirls round and round
and round.

The ride promises much, but truly delivers only a repetitive
and endless circuit. The ride goes nowhere – except in the
minds of the people who ride it and the realities of those who
keep it running. The ride is in the imagination. The ride is in
the opportunity to wave to your parents each time you circle
past their position in the crowd, to chase the horse in front of
you, and to get your picture taken.

The ride is what you bring to it.

The ride is also what you take from it.

As a carousel rider, I remember watching the ride operator
each time we circled past. He had done this job a million times,
holding the power to stop the momentum. As he finally acted,
there was that first realization that the ride was going to grind
to a halt. The horses still bobbed, but slower and slower. The
rounding still happened, but faces in the crowd lost their blur.
It was the beginning of the end. My heart sank just a smidgeon.
The wind-down seemed to take forever. Then it was over.

Over. Except it wasn't over. Because it turns out the
carousel was just one ride on the midway. All around were
other brightly colored rides with music blaring, begging to be

ridden. The world was bigger than the merry go round as long as you had tickets to ride and saw them for what they were.

On the last Thursday in November the ride operator on our merry go round touched the switch that disengaged the motor. The slow coast to a stop began for quite a few people. But it's not really the end. The memories of chasing the next horse and waving at the crowd are tucked safely away. And the midway awaits. It's over, but it's not over, because life is bigger than one ride. In fact, life is bigger than one midway.

Christmas is a hard time to see the ride operator throw the switch. But it's also the best time to remember that new life exists outside even this midway – a place we have yet to imagine. May your hope today exceed that feeling of deceleration. May your anticipation of new beginnings outweigh the momentary letdown of one ride finished.

Now it's Monday on the merry go round. But you still have tickets left to spend on the next big thing. Dig them out. Count their worth. You don't have to stop because the ride stopped. You still have what you brought to the ride, and the ride just added to what you have going forward.

Stepping off the carousel can be daunting. You might still be dizzy from the ride. But there are lots of things more exciting than a carousel out there. Monday is a great day to start something new. Get off your high horse and go find them.

Today. As a believer, you have special knowledge about these moments when life suddenly changes. You don't need to lean solely on positive thinking or a race to the next ride. You understand that the Lord of the universe, who loves you more and in better ways than you can even love yourself, officiates over the beginning and end of your every experience. He is master over the ride, the midway, and everything beyond. He gathers and He scatters – then brings you back to Him closer than you have ever been before.

The Gospel. *"Behold, the hour is coming, indeed it has come, when you will be scattered, each to his own home, and will leave me alone. Yet I am not alone, for the Father is with Me. I have said these things to you, that in Me you may have peace. In the world you will have tribulation. But take heart; I have overcome the world." John 16:32-33*

Sweet Jeans

Let us also lay aside every weight, and sin which clings so closely, and let us run with endurance the race that is set before us. Hebrews 12:1b

Reading circle was the sweetest part of second grade. That's when the teacher would glue her eyes to the pages of a book, which meant it was easy to sneak forbidden candy out of my pocket and into my mouth. I bought the candy with the money Mom gave me for milk, so it was a kind of double evil. It was great, except for those days when the teacher looked my way more often and I couldn't finish my stash. Then I had to remember to ditch the extra candy before I got home.

One day I forgot, which left a bad taste in my mother's mouth. She washed my jeans and ran them through the dryer, creating a gummed-up mess in my pocket. Not only did she make me spend hours picking out every scrap of sticky-filthy candy that clung to the fabric, but she also unearthed the fact that I had borrowed money every day from another kid to help feed my habit.

It felt bad, but it also felt good. Not only was I cleaning out the self-made mess in my inside-out pocket, but this particular sinful pattern of life no longer clung to me. It gave me an opportunity to repent. The weight was lifted, the shame was gone, and I was free to run again!

Today. Perhaps you have something that is clinging to you, and keeps you from running. It dampens your spirit, and suffocates your God-given potential. Perhaps the Spirit will convict you to repent and bring that into the light, as difficult as it might be.

The Gospel. God already knows what's in your pocket. "Repent," said Jesus many times. "Come clean. Be free to know Me." His mercies are new every morning, and they are for you. *"If you abide in My word, you are truly My disciples, and you will know the truth, and the truth will set you free." John 8:31-32*

Groovy Buttons

And while they were there, the time came for her to give birth.
And she gave birth to her firstborn son and wrapped Him
in swaddling cloths and laid Him in a manger, because
there was no place for them in the inn. Luke 2:6-7

Have you seen the Pete the Cat book series? My grandkids are mesmerized by *Pete the Cat and His Four Groovy Buttons*. The story runs like this (spoiler alert):

Pete's coat has four buttons. One pops off, but does Pete cry? "Goodness, no! Buttons come and buttons go." How many buttons are left? 4-1=3. Pete continues to lose buttons throughout the book until he reaches 1-1=0.

Then Pete discovers one more button – his belly button!

He will never lose that one. And that makes me think of this: God has a belly button, too – Jesus in the flesh.

Without a belly button, God would not have spoken to us with a human mouth. God would not have healed flesh with human hands. God would not have been offered as a perfect substitutionary sacrifice for human sin. God would not be resurrected from the human dead.

And that makes me think of this: Believers have two belly buttons! One marks flesh-birth. One marks spiritual-birth.

Your spiritual belly button marks your second birth – adoption as God's child and Jesus' brother. Like your flesh belly button it is a scar, but this scar is a reflection of Christ's wounds that made your adoption possible. You are born again.

Worldly buttons may come and go, but can Christ be subtracted from a believer's life? "Goodness, no!" His mark remains no matter what this world holds, as surely as He lives forever.

Today. Nestle into your Father's arms and remember how much He loves you today.

The Gospel. *But when the fullness of time had come, God sent forth His Son, born of woman, born under the law, to redeem those who were under the law, so that we might receive adoption as sons. Galatians 4:4-5*

Bounce

*May the God of hope fill you with all joy and peace
in believing, so that by the power of the Holy Spirit
you may abound in hope. Romans 15:13*

When I was young, I was a bounder (the type who jumps

and bounces from place to place). I had a mega-spring in my step. The kitchen table stood between our hallway and the den. Instead of going around it, I usually went over it. Our ceilings were sprinkled with hand prints.

So it came as no surprise to my mother when I discovered the sport of high jumping. In high school, I claimed the state indoor high jump record when I was a sophomore by bounding over a bar six feet, eight inches off the ground. I had "bounce."

Bounding took me places. Because I got attention for high jumping, people knew my name. I became part of the athlete social scene. I was student body vice president in a class of 600. I became those things because I bounced, not because I deserved it.

But here's the thing: I didn't create the bounce, I just had it. It was innate. I was filled with it. It sprang out of me no matter what.

That reminds me of *Acts 13:52, And the disciples were filled with joy and with the Holy Spirit.* Dear Spirit-filled Christian brother and sister, you too have bounce (the Holy Spirit within)!

Bounce is joy.
Bounce is hope.
Bounce is new life.
Bounce is endurance.
Bounce is assurance.
Bounce is freedom.
Bounce takes you places you are not otherwise qualified to go!

Today: Your identity in Christ elevates you to a position as sibling and fellow-heir to forgiveness and salvation you do not deserve. Abound in hope, for the gravity of sin no longer binds you to this earth. Leap for joy, and leave some fingerprints on the ceiling of this life!

The Gospel: Jesus' forgiveness results in abundance of joy. *Peter said, "I have no silver and gold, but what I do have I give to you. In the name of Jesus Christ of Nazareth, rise up and walk!" And he took him by the right hand and raised him up, and immediately his feet and ankles were made strong. And leaping up, he stood and began to walk, and entered the temple with them, walking and leaping and praising God. Acts 3:6-8*

Gi Whiz

*But each person is tempted when he is lured and enticed
by his own desire. James 1:14*

College is a time to explore, to discover, to break new ground. Maybe that's why I signed up for judo one semester. The only required equipment was one of those judo pajama outfits, called a gi (pronounced with a hard G and long E).

So there I was, doing P.E. in my pajamas. That worked out well, since I spent most of the time lying on the floor. The class was all about slamming people into a prone position.

Judo is called the "gentle way" because it's based on using another person's natural movements, weight and balance against him. When a person lunges in one direction, you grab and direct his movement so he can't stop going in that direction. If you anticipate your opponent properly, he always ends up on the floor.

The Bible tells us that is precisely how evil brings us

down. While Satan and his demons cannot read your mind, your perverted heart is like an open book. They observe and amplify your sinful nature to slam you down with the gentlest of tugs. You are inclined toward evil, and you fall toward those inclinations.

The inclination – our fallen nature – that is the problem! We inevitably topple to our own death. As a result, *"No one does good, not even one." Romans 3:12b*

Understanding sin's judo-like characteristics is the only way to come to the end of ourselves and come to Christ. It is what makes us treasure Christ so dearly – our only Mediator. *See 1 Timothy 2:5.* It is our only guard against moving so quickly to lunge at our fallen hearts' affections.

Today. *Be sober-minded; be watchful. Your adversary the devil prowls around like a roaring lion, seeking someone to devour. 1 Peter 5:8* Lean today on your only hope, the sovereign Christ – whose power equips you to stand and whose mercies pick you up when you fall.

The Gospel. Good news! Satan may be a Gi Whiz, but God is by far the Gi Whizziest. God is the Master of using balance against a foe, as He demonstrated by the cross-sacrifice that crushed Satan to the ground in eternal defeat. *See Colossians 2:13-15.*

True
Freedom

Guilt that Leads to Hurt
Lies that Lead to a Prison
Repentance that Leads to Liberty
God's Work that Leads the Hurting Home

Guilt
that Leads to Hurt

For my life is spent with sorrow, and my years with sighing;
my strength fails because of my iniquity,
and my bones waste away. Psalm 31:10

Another late night on a lonely road, and there was that voice again: "Kill yourself."

The rumbling lullaby of a short block 350 motor kept coaxing my eyelids downward. That, and the monotonous rumble of the Michelins on the pavement. Focus, man. Shake your head hard. Keep those eyes open.

November 1976. My 1955 Chevy pickup and I had made this trip together countless times. So very familiar, this stretch of Interstate 35 between Austin (University of Texas) and Fort Worth (girlfriend and home). A familiar road, and that familiar suggestion to escape this life.

I cranked up the 8-track tape player and tried to drown out the voice. I looked for distractions, running my hands across the burnt-orange bench seat of the truck. No relief there. I hated that fresh padding and perfect stitching. I glanced up at the new headliner, another tangible reminder of my guilt. One by one, the miles passed.

"Just drive across the median. Hit a car."

The voice kept nagging, more insistent than the doleful tunes of Willie Nelson. I stroked the finely finished wood handle of the fancy chrome floor shifter. It gave me chills. Oncoming headlights gleamed off the flawless orange paint of the hood. My gloom intensified.

"You're in too deep. That's what shame feels like."

The voice was right. Its accusations heaped up day after day, night after night, until I could no longer see around them. How did I ever get into this mess? Hopeless. Endless. Numbing. It was true of this drive, true of my life. I hated that truck.

Today. Have you ever felt that way? Have you ever come to the end of your rope? Maybe you are there right now. Hang on. There's hope.

The Gospel. We cannot come to repentance unless God produces in us a grief for who and what we are as sinners. His redeeming work begins with the gift of eyes to see our desperate need. *For godly grief produces a repentance that leads to salvation without regret, whereas worldly grief produces death. 2 Corinthians 7:10*

Lies
that Lead to a Prison

*The iniquities of the wicked ensnare him, and he is held fast
in the cords of his sin. He dies for lack of discipline,
and because of his great folly he is led astray. Proverbs 5:22-23*

I didn't always hate my truck. In fact, I started out loving her more than anything.

In high school we kids shared one of the family's cars, then I bummed rides my first year of college. So I was a sophomore before I got wheels of my own. All I could afford was a 20-year-old rusty pickup that said "For Sale, $275" in the back window. Of course, it needed a little work, but it was mine. It was love at first sight.

One summer I worked for a soft drink company, where family friends owned and managed the operation. Every day I drove a fully-loaded truck out to the company's parking lot and sold cases of soft drinks to church groups, convenience store owners, and anybody else authorized to buy wholesale.

A guy who sits in a parking lot all day has time to think. What he thinks about says a lot about what his heart treasures the most. This guy thought a lot about his truck, strategically parked where he could see it all day. This guy thought, "That truck could use some paint. That truck could use better suspension. That truck could use . . . ."

You could say I idolized that truck. What I did that summer proves I did. It worked like this:

Sometimes people needed more soft drinks than I had with me in the parking lot, especially around holidays. So I retrieved more cases from the warehouse and added them to my beginning inventory. At day's end I reconciled the truck like any truck route driver, matching up dollars received and inventory sold.

One day I failed to mark some added cases to my beginning inventory. When you do that, you come up with extra cash at day's end. At first it hurts your conscience to stick that cash in your pocket, but it hurts less the next day, and the next. Soon it became no problem to pay for work done on my idol with thousands of dollars stolen from work. Bodywork, paint, interior, motor, transmission. It was looking good.

I went to church. I read my Bible. I prayed. But my heart was out in the truck. Pride. Self-sufficiency. Insatiable desires for more, no matter the cost.

Bad heart-habits are hard to break, even if you want to. In Austin, I landed a job as cashier at a retailer. I shared the register with others, but it was still possible to slip a few dollars out of the tray once in a while. Then I came back to Fort Worth and spent another summer selling soft drinks in the parking lot.

That's when that destructive voice of conscience began – the one that kept nagging me on lonely, late-night drives. I came home every other weekend, so the voice was plenty familiar by Thanksgiving 1976. But on that particular holiday drive it was more insistent than ever.

"It's hopeless. Kill yourself."

Today. Have you ever wondered how you got trapped in some mess? Do you wonder how you fell for Satan's lie, which has become your prison? It's a hard, scary place to be. The thing you loved now locks you up and rules you. Maybe it's your hidden dungeon of pornography, jealousy, seething anger, or . . . .

The Gospel. Satan's whispers always lead us to places that lead to destruction – on paths that lead away from our only true Source of Life, Jesus Christ. The Good News is that our Source of Life pursues us. Our hopelessness is visible only by the light God shines, and our freedom is possible only through the blood Jesus shed.

Repentance
that Leads to Liberty

From that time Jesus began to preach, saying,
"Repent, for the kingdom of heaven is at hand." Matthew 4:17
I acknowledged my sin to You, and I did not cover My iniquity;
I said, "I will confess my transgressions to the LORD,"
and You forgave the iniquity of my sin. Psalm 32:5

By God's grace and will, I drove on that night. He protected me from the voice, and I made the journey to Fort Worth safely.

But the next night, while I was watching TV at my girlfriend's house, a spiritual showdown occurred. God had enough of my divided heart. In His time and His way He finally crushed me with conviction, so much so I suddenly collapsed into heaps of uncontrollable sobbing. God's sorrow became my sorrow. The story could no longer hide. It took a long time to choke out the truth to my bewildered girlfriend.

Confession. It was the only exit from my hardened heart, and God caused it to open. God drove me to confess to my shocked parents. I confessed to my dumbfounded pastor. I confessed to my astonished employers, who mercifully pressed no charges. But most of all I confessed to God – the Person whose holiness stood in stark contrast to my own stained soul.

By God's grace, He moved my heart to repentance – not to escape the worldly consequences of my sin, but because it was God's way of tearing down the bars that held me captive. He lanced a deep wound, and drained out the ugly. He shined light into my darkest recesses. As a result He did the impossible: He restored my fellowship with Him.

There were consequences, of course. They hurt. I left the Austin college scene and returned to Fort Worth. I left the apartment life to live at home. I sold the truck. I licked my wounded reputation. And most of what I earned during the next several years went to my former employers.

But the voice was gone. In its place was that *"peace which passes understanding." Philippians 4:7* It felt so good to come home. I knew just how that prodigal son felt in Luke 15. My parents did, too.

Conviction, repentance, confession, and restoration. That cycle is God's precious gift for believers, the only exit from the sinful places our hearts can take us. That cycle is possible only because Jesus exchanges His righteousness for each sinner who comes to beg Him for it.

You may find yourself thinking your heart is too deeply off course for this to apply. You may feel ashamed of some things. You may hear an accuser's voice suggesting you are hopeless. Don't let these things hold you captive. Christ came to set you free. Take the exit that only He provides. Thank Him for revealing your heart to you. He didn't have to, you know.

Today. Have you ever felt the sudden release of sin's

unbearable accusations? Praise God! Only Jesus' sacrifice makes it possible. Only God's mercy makes it applicable. Confession and forgiveness. It's the best feeling in the world, because it is God's voice saying, "Welcome home."

The Gospel. *There is therefore now no condemnation for those who are in Christ Jesus. For the law of the Spirit of life has set you free in Christ Jesus from the law of sin and death. Romans 8:1-2*

God's Work that Leads the Hurting Home

Rejoice in hope, be patient in tribulation, be constant in prayer. Romans 12:12

In this chapter I have shared a true story about one of the darkest periods in my life. Faced with guilt for stealing thousands of dollars, I finally collapsed under the pressure. God compelled me to turn myself in – to my girlfriend, my parents, my pastor, and the companies I stole from. I lost my job, my reputation, and my independence. It took several years to repay the companies while I moved back home and finished college.

But that's not the whole story!

Two weeks before my story reached its climax, a middle-aged couple slipped quietly into the pews at a Fort Worth church. The surroundings were familiar; for more than 25 years they had worshiped there. They had faithfully raised a family there, bringing two sons and a daughter through the Sunday School.

This particular night, a special service for healing was in progress. The couple was not infirm. Perhaps they came with his aging father in mind. Like others in the congregation, they were asked to write their healing need on a 3x5 card.

When it was their turn, the couple rose from their pew and made their way up the aisle to an area in front of the altar. They handed their card to the two pastors, who laid hands on their heads and prayed for the healing they desired.

As the pastors read the card, they noticed that the couple was not praying for a physical healing of any sort. The card simply said,

"For our family."

The words of their prayer for the healing of a family that night echoed off the marble floor, resonating past the richly carved wood of the church and into the highest reaches of the sanctuary and beyond. It mirrored their own ongoing, urgent prayers, casting their cares on the only source of redemption, hope and change.

Mom and Dad were there that night. My parents were the couple who prayed for a healed family, even as my soul was mired in a secret and dark prison they didn't know about. As they drove home, their prayer lay before God's heart and worked its way into His sovereign plan.

Two weeks later I was healed and came home. I was set free. I was restored to my family and God, cleansed of my guilt, and given a clean bill of spiritual health by God Himself.

Once buried in despair, I was suddenly resurrected in hope. As painful as it was, I rejoiced then and today that God lifted my life out of quicksand and placed it again on a solid Rock.

Today. If you still see Jesus as only an example of good deeds and lover of whatever path you choose, and believe in God only to satisfy your own selfish longings, I pray He opens your eyes. That "Jesus" has no power to deal with your sins when your earthly days are spent and you are confronted with God's holiness.*

If you have run to Jesus as Son of God – sacrificial offering for your sins, exchanging His life for yours on the cross so that His righteous life has become your life – and you have still fallen prey to Satan's deceitful whispers, I pray that He brings you to that same crushing moment I experienced. May He bring you to repentance and the liberty you yearn for.

If you have simply "lost your first love" for Christ, as John reports of one church in Revelation 2, I pray God will rekindle your affections for Him. May your passion for Christ and His ways burst into flames, consuming every other passion that besets you.

The Gospel. *[God] has delivered us from the domain of darkness and transferred us to the kingdom of His beloved Son, in whom we have redemption, the forgiveness of sins. Colossians 1:13-14*

*Perhaps you are asking, "How can I know this life-saving, hurt-comforting Jesus? How can I know this hope of heaven?" I would encourage you to turn to page 144 for the answer.

Hurt
Hope
Heaven

Hurting in Death: Garry's Story
Healing in Forgiveness: Daniel's Story
A Final Word: It's Okay to Cry
A Prayer for the Hurting

Hurting in Death: Garry's Story

Leukemia. My brother-in-law's diagnosis came out of the blue. It sent Garry and his wife, Loyce, into a numbing series of decisions and a brutal round of chemotherapy and other treatments. Complications soon sent him into the ICU, but there was no reason to think he would not endure through the treatments as so many others have.

In the meantime, Garry hurt. The hurtest I saw him was about 10 days into his treatment. His body was in severe pain on many levels, and internal sores denied every attempt to eat, drink or even speak plainly. Infection and lack of nutrition were taking their toll. Tears welled up in his eyes, the understandable display of agony that would not stop. But there was more to it than that.

Slowly typing words into his phone, Garry spelled out the source of his deepest misery to his dear wife, who had stuck by his side hour after hour: Garry was crushed that he had become so short with her that day, that he had kept hurting his "best friend" with his words and actions. While she assured him that they were bearing these burdens together, and he had also been there for her when she hurt so badly, his confession was not misplaced. At some level of testing he was found to be sinful – as we all are.

Garry's hopelessness in his own ability to perfectly love and act was turned over to Jesus Christ many years ago. The Savior convicted him and drew him to a grace that atoned for every sin past, present and future. Garry knew God's forgiveness, without which he could not enter heaven someday. Loyce knew that same forgiveness, which she was able to offer Garry time after time. Where the law produced guilt, the Son purchased freedom by His sacrifice of Himself on the cross for our law-breaking. Garry lived in that hope.

Then Garry died.

Suddenly. Unexpectedly. Two weeks after his diagnosis, Garry's heart gave out on a Saturday evening. A team of the most skilled and compassionate doctors and nurses imaginable rushed into his room with focused passion and action. For 45 minutes they fought against his body's effort to shut down. Then the room became silent. Except for sobs. Except for whispers. Except for a reverence for the sanctity of a man's life.

The team quietly withdrew to reserve time and space for the family. So much said, but also so much wanting to be said. So many prayers answered, but so many prayers now clearly denied by the God who held Garry's life and death in His hands. So many unanswered questions – except for the one thing we knew.

Garry was alive.

In a moment that broke our hearts the promises of God were also fulfilled as only God could fulfill them.

Death inevitably claims each person at some age. But life – that is another matter. Real life comes only to those who come to the end of their own self-reliance, cry out to Christ as their sin-sacrifice, and receive His love on His terms.

Garry's body was left defenseless by his leukemia. But Garry's spirit – that was another matter. In an instant Garry was made new and his torment exchanged for peace everlasting. Jesus' blood also flowed in Garry's veins – life-saving blood that carried our dearly beloved brother into the Savior's arms.

Garry embraced the Gospel, stated here in *Romans 5: But God shows His love for us in that while we were still sinners, Christ died for us. Since, therefore, we have now been justified by His blood, much more shall we be saved by Him from the wrath of God. For if while we were enemies we were reconciled to God by the death of His Son, much more, now that we are reconciled, shall we be saved by His life. More than that, we also rejoice in God through our Lord Jesus Christ, through whom we have now received reconciliation.*

Garry was hurting like hell. But that hurt had a balm, the hope of heaven. That hope in Christ gave him a reason to press on in this world with faith, and to enter the next world with thanksgiving. His life, labor, and hurting were not in vain so long as they provided a window into God's grace for the world. Neither is yours.

The Gospel. *When the perishable puts on the imperishable, and the mortal puts on immortality, then shall come to pass the saying that is written:*

"Death is swallowed up in victory."

"O death, where is your victory?

O death, where is your sting?"

The sting of death is sin, and the power of sin is the law. But thanks be to God, who gives us the victory through our Lord Jesus Christ. Therefore, my beloved brothers, be steadfast, immovable, always abounding in the work of the Lord, knowing that in the Lord your labor is not in vain. 1 Corinthians 15:54-58

Healing in Forgiveness: Daniel's Story

Nearly 20 family members were sitting down to supper at my house when the phone rang. The call left me numb.

. . . Daniel

. . . was in an accident

. . . and he's dead.

The voice was both devastated and stoic, and my mind refused to process the information. I was still in denial as Bill gave me a location. I was barely able to keep my composure as I whispered the news to my wife and rushed out the door.

Bill and Laura had two children, 18-year-old Daniel and his older sister, Emily. The Lord had knit them together like few families I knew. Daniel had been alone in a car, headed downtown to join some others from our church to talk about Jesus to people on the streets.

When I reached the scene a handful of others were already there with Bill. We were told that a drunk driver had been traveling at a high rate of speed, lost control of his truck, and plowed into the driver's side of Daniel's car. The police had taped a barrier 100 yards from the wreckage. Only Bill was allowed to make the long, lonely walk to a place where he could see the severely crushed vehicles. He was told that his son had died instantly. The drunk walked away.

We huddled in a lonely place that night, surrounded by flashing emergency lights and sirens, remembering a son who was gone and hugging the parents who ached. We kept reminding each other that a loving Father was still holding the universe together, a Spirit was praying with groanings too deep for words, and a Son had called a young man home on his way to telling other people about that Son.

Word spread rapidly and Bill and Laura's house was soon packed with people. For a very long time we prayed, we cried, we read scripture. Finally we left the family alone to miss Daniel as only a broken family could. The following night they sat in the front pew of the church as people offered words of comfort and read scriptures of hope to them.

Then came the funeral. What Daniel was not able to say on the streets of downtown Fort Worth that night, many unbelievers willingly listened to at his celebration of life, in the clearest and most expansive presentation of the Gospel I have ever heard.

The time since those days has been unimaginably hard for Daniel's family. They truly walked through the valley of the shadow of death.

Yet they had the deepest desire and God-blessed strength to do the unthinkable. They forgave the man who killed their son. First they forgave him before God. Then Bill was able to stand up and speak the Gospel directly to that man and express their forgiveness publicly as he was sentenced in court. *As the Lord has forgiven you, so you also must forgive. Colossians 3:13b*

Somehow they have made it through the ensuing years of birthdays and holidays. They still visit Daniel's memory at his grave and make family trips to the vacation spots where so many memories were built together. But everywhere they go they take the sustaining power of God in Christ. He has faithfully walked them through every step, speaking to them through tears, laughter, scripture, books, sermons, and the prayers and encouragement of the saints.

Today. *Therefore, since we are surrounded by so great a cloud of witnesses, let us also lay aside every weight, and sin which clings so closely, and let us run with endurance the race that is set before us, looking to Jesus, the founder and perfecter of our faith, who for the joy that was set before Him endured the cross, despising the shame, and is seated at the right hand of the throne of God. Hebrews 12:1-2*

The Gospel. I wonder what it would be like to be the father in Bill's shoes. Bill himself reminds me that his ultimate Comforter experienced the same thing, even more so: another Father was separated from His Son. They were close, very close. The Son was on a mission to tell people about salvation. Law breakers killed Him, drunk with their own self-righteousness. Then Christ's blood made forgiveness possible.

That is the Gospel. That is forgiveness. That is life, even in hurt. Even in death. Even for you.

A Final Word:
It's Okay to Cry

You have kept count of my tossings; put my tears in Your bottle.
Are they not in Your book? Psalm 56:8

Dawn was just breaking at a men's retreat one clear March morning, that hour when the dewy landscape is dotted with guys and their Bibles seeking rural communion with their Maker.

Like others, I was contemplating the sunrise and what God would tell me that weekend when my cell phone interrupted the moment. The news rocked my world. The 19-year-old daughter of dear friends had died while serving in Iraq.

Sitting there on a concrete retaining wall, I felt a family's pain. It stabbed so deep that I cried for half an hour before gathering my gear and heading home.

That wasn't the only time I cried.

I remember the day I fired my best friend. He worked for my company, which was struggling to keep pace with expenses. My friend and I both knew that his position was overpaid and no longer critical. I took a long walk the night before, searching my soul. The next day I called him in. As such meetings should be, it was short and to the point. We parted as friends, loving and respecting each other. But I remember the hurt, nonetheless. That evening, I sat down on the edge of my bed and collapsed in sobs that seemed to last forever. He may have done the same.

We cried then. I still cry about things that hurt.

I want to be clear about something as you reach the last

pages of this book. It's okay to express your hurt, sorrow, and grief. It's okay to cry.

I was about to spend time with someone I know recently. Some hard news was fresh on her mind. "I think I'd like to stay home," she said.

"Would you like me to keep you company?" I asked.

"No," she responded. "I just haven't gotten to cry yet."

Crying doesn't mean that you don't have enough faith. Crying doesn't mean you are failing at joy. Crying doesn't mean the devil has won. Crying doesn't mean that God is suddenly frowning on you.

Crying means that you are sad. Crying means that you are up close and personal with the world's broken parts. Crying often means that you are sharing God's perspective on creation, experiencing His lamentations.

Jesus wept over the lost as He approached Jerusalem. *See Luke 19.* Jesus wept at the idea of a family's sorrow in death. *See John 11.* Peter wept over His denial of Christ. *See Matthew 26.* Mary Magdalene wept at Jesus' tomb. *See John 20.*

Today. It's okay to cry. It's okay to hope. It's okay to cry and hope at the same time.

The Gospel. *[God] will swallow up death forever; and the Lord God will wipe away tears from all faces, and the reproach of His people He will take away from all the earth, for the Lord has spoken. Isaiah 25:8*

A Prayer
for the Hurting

Our Father in heaven, whose name is Care and Comfort and who superintends this world You made with a passion and tenderness that far exceed our understanding, we find ourselves at a loss in our own understanding of Your ways.

We acutely feel the effects of that moment when sin entered Your creation and broke the perfect peace, solemnity and joy that were once present. We hurt. Even as we are committed to trusting You in every way, we are also prone to anger. Our grief or shock threatens to overwhelm us in every dimension, threatening our own perspective and faith and health.

How can numbness and pain be so very simultaneous? Why can't we muster enough energy to even move?

Please uphold us with Your mighty Hand, even as these waves pound us. Remind us that You know the end from the beginning and You are using all things to bring ultimate glory to Yourself and Your ways – that You see behind the curtain that we cannot. Be our assurance that even the troubles of this world are worth enduring because they are part of Your elegant tapestry which will someday display the fullness of Your goodness and beauty. You have specifically chosen to make us a part of Your handiwork.

Remind us that we can be sure that You have not forgotten or forsaken us, though circumstances may twist our minds that way. Instead, You have already demonstrated that the opposite is true. You have given of Yourself in such horrible human ways that we are equally unable to understand it. You have delivered Your own body over to the crushing effects of sin in the world – willingly, lovingly – that our own lives may be saved for eternity. While we were still sinners and radically unlovable, You loved us and died for us.

Thank You that we will live to see Your work completed, and even today's hurt will be seen in the light of Your eternal perspective. Amen.

Child of God, may His peace which passes all understanding hold you tightly. Fall into His arms and lay all your feelings at His feet. Let Him address them one by one in His time. Wherever and however darkness clouds your way, may Christ prove Himself strong to be your Light.

The Source
of Hope

Throughout this book I have referred to the hope of heaven, which comes through Jesus Christ. I have punctuated each story with something called the Gospel, which means "good news." The good news is this: that freedom from sin's grip on your life is within reach. It is held in God's hand – marked by His perfect sacrifice of blood on the cross, substituting His righteous life for yours. And it is offered to you as a free gift.

At this point, you may wonder, "How do I take hold of that gift?" *If you confess with your mouth that Jesus is Lord and believe in your heart that God raised Him from the dead, you will be saved. Romans 10:9* You come to the end of yourself and confess your need for Jesus to God and to the world. You live a life that reflects a belief in the earth-shattering, finished work of Jesus crucified for your sins.

Jesus knew hurt in ways we never will and offers comfort that no other can. He is the hope of heaven. *Now to Him who is able to keep you from stumbling and to present you blameless before the presence of His glory with great joy, to the only God, our Savior, through Jesus Christ our Lord, be glory, majesty, dominion, and authority, before all time and now and forever. Amen. Jude 24-25*

About the Author

One Christmas morning in elementary school, young Michael Branch was surprised with a gift he never thought to ask for but loved at first sight. Under the tree he found an old mechanical typewriter, rescued by Santa from a repair shop to make the holiday seem fuller on a family's tight budget.

That providential gift inspired a job in newspapers, a career in magazines, and a tool to point to the glories of God through the true stories found in life's everyday moments.

He and his wife have four children and umpteen grandchildren, all of whom God uses to make their daily lives richer and their knowledge of Him fuller.

Made in the USA
Middletown, DE
02 December 2017